GREAT IS YOUR REWARD

Books by Norman K. Elliott:

HOW TO BE THE LORD'S PRAYER
GREAT IS YOUR REWARD

GREAT

IS YOUR

REWARD

LIVING THE BEATITUDES

Norman K. Elliott

FLEMING H. REVELL COMPANY
WESTWOOD · NEW JERSEY

Acknowledgment is made to Putnam's & Conrad-McCann for "Each in His Own Tongue" by William H. Carruth, from *Each in His Own Tongue and Other Poems*. Used by permission.

Scripture quotations in this publication, unless otherwise identified, are from the *Revised Standard Version of the Bible*, copyrighted 1946 and 1952, by the Division of Christian Education, National Council of Churches, and used by permission.

Acknowledgment

This book could not have been written without the help and encouragement of the following friends:

Mrs. Fred S. Markham, who made it possible for me to record the first draft into a portable tape recorder; Mrs. George Suzuki, who contributed typing, clear criticism, and suggestions concerning the manuscript; Mrs. Helen McGovern and Mrs. Ruby Roskilly, whose help in reading and criticism has been invaluable; my friend, Frank D. Randolph, whose encouragement and persistence inspired me to begin the book when I did; above all, my wife Marion, who offered inspiration and the sharing of ideas, help in editing the manuscript, and, most important, her general ability to keep me working.

All these have made the book possible, and to each and all I wish to express my deep gratitude.

Norman K. Elliott

Preface

The beatitudes of Jesus encompass the whole range of human aspiration:

how to possess the Kingdom of Heaven
how to find comfort
how to inherit the earth
how to find satisfaction
how to obtain mercy
how to see God
how to be the sons of God
how to be one with the prophets.

Quite a list of aspirations, indeed, broad enough to include the goals of every man. Not every man seeks them all, but certainly all who are born into this life want and need some of them.

Therefore the beatitudes of Jesus are guidelines, methods, means, and insights by which a man may attain fulfillment, happiness, and wholeness.

The beatitudes are tied together by one word, "blessed." There is no doubt, judging from their content, and also from Jesus' own life, that what is "blessed" is the condition of community with God, the Author and Sustainer of life, and the results of such community. Thus the beatitudes are signposts and directions for developing a sense of oneness with all life, achieving the richness of full living, and satisfying the purpose of human existence.

The word we have translated "blessed," comes from the Greek word *makarios;* the usual definition of this Greek word is "happy" or "fortunate."

On the surface, it seems difficult to equate all the beatitudes with being happy. It makes no sense to say, "Happy are those who mourn," or "Happy are the persecuted." Yet there is a deeper level of meaning at which the word "happiness" can include even these. Even the mournful and the persecuted are in a happy or providential state if their condition results in their finding fulfillment. Perhaps "fortunate" is a more applicable word. The mournful and the persecuted may well be in a fortunate condition if it leads them to something laudable and strong and clean.

The happy or fortunate aspect of tragedy comes about when the unhappiness leads to God. A woman in the crowd once cried out to Jesus, "Blessed is the womb that bore you, and the breasts that you sucked!" Jesus quickly answered, "Blessed rather are those who hear the word of God and keep it!" (LUKE 11:27, 28).

How often, and with what constancy, He turned the minds of His listeners to God! Not even when people wanted to make Him a king, did he waver. The work He had given Himself to offered no compromise. God, and the life with God, were all that mattered.

There is no question but that a life centered in God, dedicated to God, fed by God, given to God, and in communion with God was Jesus' conception of being blessed. There is no doubt, either, that such a life, locked in conjunction with God, bore its fruits; it was related to the problems of everyday living. A life in God, and one dedicated to Him, would show results.

Jesus told a parable in the home of a Pharisee who had invited Him to dinner, and it indicates His recognition that efforts expended have their reward. "When you give a dinner or a banquet, do not invite your friends or your brothers or your kinsmen or rich neighbors, lest they also invite you in return, and you be repaid. But when you give a feast, invite the poor, the maimed, the lame, the blind, and you will be blessed, because they cannot repay you. You will be repaid at the resurrection of the just" (LUKE 14:12-14).

More enlightening still is what Jesus said to Peter: "Truly, I say to you, there is no one who has left house or brothers or sisters or mother or father or children or lands, for my sake and for the gospel, who will not receive a hundredfold now in this time, houses and brothers and sisters and mothers and children and lands, with persecutions, and in the age to come eternal life" (MARK 10:29, 30).

Two things are emphasized here, and undoubtedly related: a life in God will find its rewards here, and it will also know its rewards in the hereafter.

Clearly, then, those who are blessed are not going to wander through this world like destitute orphans, or like prisoners on some sort of Devil's Island, cut off from the normal rewards of living. They will know the fruits of their efforts here, as well as in heaven.

There are two aspects of the word "blessed" which ought to be noted. The blessed are those who are dedicated to God, committed to His way of life, enlisted in efforts to bring life on earth into harmony with God's intention, and who find companionship and communion with God. The blessed are the *dedicated*, the *committed*, the *enlisted*, and the *companions* of God.

However, the blessed are also those who are in a condition to receive the life and nature of God. Divine graces flow more readily toward and through the person who is blessed. He is able to find the answer to his life's quest, the satisfaction of his heart's desires, and the solution to his problems. Such a man is blessed, in a state of blessedness, or in the condition where blessedness can happen to him. For example, when the person who mourns discovers the God of all comforts, his sorrow has not only put him in a position to receive the strength of God, but also to experience the nature of that blessedness.

The blessed man reveals God wherever he is. Those in his company find themselves reminded of God, aware of God, or in the presence of God. When Jesus performed a miracle, it is said that the people praised God. God revealed Himself through the vehicle of Jesus' personality. We may not understand how it happens, but we know that the experience is real.

A good friend of mine, an Episcopal priest, came into the Christian life in a most remarkable way. He had been reared in a home that had nothing to do with the church. He knew that there were churches, but he did not know what went on in them. When he was transferred from New York City to Reno, Nevada, he met a very dedicated Christian girl, and they were married. When the children were born, my friend saw that his wife was not too happy with a nonchurch life.

"I know that you want the children reared in the church," he told her. "Visit churches, and wherever you want to go, that's all right with me. In fact, I'll help you look for one."

So, for the first time in his life, George went to church. Finally he and his wife settled on an Episcopal church, and had a conference with the elderly priest in charge.

"I thought he was crazy," George told me later. "He was

talking about somebody being the Son of God. I had never heard such talk in my life. But there was one thing about that priest that did impress me—*he believed it!* And even though it sounded crazy to me, I went along with it because there was something about him that I could not deny."

Well, George did join the church, and after a few years began to study for the ministry. Today he is a good pastor and a man of God. And it all came about because he met a man in whom *God shone through.*

The blessed have placed all the possibilities of human personality at God's disposal, to do with as He sees fit. God reveals Himself through their bodies, their whole personalities. They have been changed. Yes, they still are human, they still exhibit their natural characteristics, but something more has been added. They have not lost their personality, and yet, in a sense, they have. The elements that make up the human personality have been regrouped in them, and transformed into a new personality.

One young priest came back to his hometown church to preach his first sermon, and one of the congregation said, "I don't know what has happened, but *something* has! I've known this boy since he was a little tot. I never knew this was in him."

Well, maybe it was in him—*in potential*—but it took God to put it all together in a new way.

A man given to profanity came into the presence of God in the personality of Rufus Moseley. He told me later, "I just couldn't talk in the way. I usually do. There is something about this man that made me know I was with a holy man, a man close to God."

Such are the blessed. They are the windows, in human form, that God shines through.

The beatitudes of Jesus pull aside the thin veil that separates man from his true destiny. When rightly understood and applied, they lead us into that oneness with life, with God, which holds the answer to all the riddles of the world. This is what Edward Carpenter expresses so beautifully in these lines:

So Thin a Veil

So thin a veil divides
Us from such joy, past words,
Walking in daily life—the business of the hour, each detail
    seen to;
Yet carried, rapt away, on what sweet floods of other Being:
Swift streams of music flowing, light far back through all
    Creation shining,
Loved faces looking—
Ah! from the true, the mortal self
So thin a veil divides!

NORMAN K. ELLIOTT

Contents

GREAT IS YOUR REWARD

1
The Poor in Spirit

Blessed are the poor in spirit, for theirs is the kingdom of heaven—MATTHEW 5:3

THE poor in spirit are the poor in ego. The ego is that something which enables a man to say "I," and in the very process of doing this, separating and differentiating himself from everything else in the universe. "I" automatically means "not you, nor you, nor you—nor anything else in the world!" The ego emphasizes that which makes the individual unique. Without the ego, man would experience identity with all creation. Absence of ego enabled St. Francis to say, "Brother fire, sister water," and so forth. The more ego we have, the less oneness and identity we feel with our fellow man, with the universe, and ultimately with God.

One of the chief ways in which modern psychology differs from the insight of Jesus is in the treatment of the ego. Modern psychology seeks to emphasize and strengthen the ego, whereas Jesus counseled us to lose it. However, one does not lose the ego merely by concentrating upon losing it. The only way is to become interested in and attracted by a force so overwhelming and overpowering that it becomes the center around which the personality is integrated in a new way.

Jesus reminded us that a man would find his life only in losing it. By finding his life we assume He means that a man will be able to release all the potentialities for great living which lie dormant within him. It is not unusual to become so interested in something else that we forget ourselves. In the involvement, in the forgetting about ourselves, we are able to achieve more and enjoy more than we could by any other means. There is nothing more satisfying and thrilling than to find ourselves absorbed in a work that envelopes us with a sense of oneness.

Few sights are more thrilling than a basketball team that suddenly "catches fire." Each man, without consciously thinking about it, is automatically in the right place at the right time. It seems that each player is able to score from any place on the court. Five personalities are acting as one, and the results are thrilling. This is only possible when each individual loses himself, and is absorbed into something greater than his own ego.

We are drawn to whatever we are looking at, or emphasizing in our thoughts. If we concentrate upon ourselves, upon our ego, our personality is integrated around that ego no matter how small it might be.

A friend of mine likes to ride a bicycle. When he moved to a new neighborhood, he found that there was a tree halfway down a certain hill which he had to avoid. In the beginning, he looked at the tree each time he started down the hill. However, he tells me that after hitting the tree a few times he learned the great secret of looking at something else.

When my bicycle-riding friend looked at something else,

he was drawn to it. Exactly the same thing can be said for the human personality. My friend discovered that the way to miss a tree was to pick out another target and keep his eyes on it. When he did this, the tree seemed to take care of itself. So it is with the ego. Fall in love with something attractive enough and interesting enough, and the problem of the ego will take care of itself. The human personality will then be integrated around a new center.

Pride is the result of ego, its twin brother. The one who is proud refers everything to himself. As far as he is concerned, the whole universe revolves around his interests. Pride separates him from everybody else, and it separates everybody else from him. Actually, the separation is in his own mind. His pride is the result of sin, or separation.

In the Old Testament, the prophet tells us that it is *our* sin which has separated us from God. The implication is that God has never separated Himself from us. We are the ones, because of our pride and ego, who do the separating, and therefore let ourselves in for difficulties.

Childlikeness, on the other hand, is the fruit of being poor in spirit. A child naturally identifies himself with everything, from a ray of sunlight streaming through the window to the stranger who happens to come into the home. The child remains this way until he is taught to act like an adult, which often means to emphasize his own ego.

A good friend of mine who lives in Dallas, Texas, tells of an incident in his own life which illustrates the power of being poor in spirit, and finding out that the Kingdom of Heaven is here all the time. This man had been a road contractor when the Depression struck and he was wiped out. Others in his position declared bankruptcy to escape the burden of unimaginable debts, but this man decided not to do so. He felt he had an obligation to those who had backed him financially. Against the advice of friends and lawyers, he decided to try and weather the storm. He was inundated by debt.

One day he was walking along the street and came face to face with a banker. All pride had gone. He had been trusting, reaching out and yearning for something which would make his world fall into place once more. Suddenly, without forethought, he nodded to the banker, stopped, and heard himself saying, "How would you like to back a broken-down contractor?"

The banker was so startled and intrigued by this honesty and humility that he asked my friend to step into the bank and talk the matter over. The result was that the banker arranged to back a "broken-down contractor."

Over a long period of time the debts were paid off, and my friend went on to become very successful. Because pride had vanished, because he had become poor in spirit, lacking in ego, my friend was able to enter the Kingdom of Heaven and to possess the rewards of that Kingdom.

When Jesus rode into Jerusalem on a little donkey, the crowds shouted, "Hosanna; blessed is he that cometh in the name of the Lord" (MARK 11:9, KJV). Had he ridden into the capital city on a beautiful white stallion, or on a magnificent Arabian charger, the crowds might have said, "Look at the beautiful horse!" Because the little donkey was so insignificant, Jesus and His purpose were magnified. And, because Jesus was magnified, the little donkey has lived in history. In losing his life, the little animal found it.

We have no need to fear that we will miss the benefits of perfect living if we so lose ourselves. On the contrary, we shall reap the benefits of living in perfect relationship with

· 22 ·

all creation, simply because we have lost ourselves, or be-come poor in spirit. The Kingdom of Heaven is the King-dom of Right Relationships; ultimately this is God and the expression of God in the universe.

Being in right relationship with all things will automat-ically mean that the good things of life will spontaneously flow toward us, and we will flow toward the good things of life.

The humble, or the poor in spirit, are those who are trans-parent. Only the egoist needs to hide behind the mask of hypocrisy. Dag Hammarskjold, in his book *Markings*, says that humility is complete self-effacement.

Self-effacement! What a perfect description of the poor in spirit! Jesus was so *poor in spirit* that the people saw only God in Him. Jesus was so much *not there* that the multitudes were only aware of God the Father. And, be-cause of the poorness of spirit of Jesus, God visited mankind as He has never done before—nor since.

Notice the words of the beatitude that "theirs *is* the kingdom of heaven." It does not say that they *have* the Kingdom of Heaven, but rather that they *are* the Kingdom of Heaven. This would have to be so, because in *erasing* the ego they are adjusted to that system and pattern of relation-ships in the universe which is expressed as the Kingdom of Heaven.

There is a story about Redcap 42 which illustrates how the poor in spirit come into right relationship with others on earth. A man working with Redcap 42 had been teasing him for some weeks about his faith in Christ. Night after night Redcap 42 went home knowing that his tormentor was getting the better of him. He was nervous, and his patience had worn thin. One day he could endure it no longer. All his defenses were down, and he blurted out, "All right, all right. I know that I am not all that I claim for my faith and my Lord, but I'm doing the best I can!"

Redcap 42 had gone beyond the point of trying to impress anybody. He was childlike and transparent. He had thrown himself on the mercy of his antagonist. This sheer honesty, this poorness of spirit which admitted failure, so impressed the other man that he became interested in the Christian life. Had Redcap 42 tried to bluster his way out of the situation with pride, his antagonist would have recognized it immediately and gone his way convinced that religion was just so much fakery. However, the genuineness of the reaction, the complete self-transparency, was evidence that Redcap 42 had something which his adversary wanted.

In the Kingdom of Right Relationships the humble man can transform that which is bad into something good. This is the Kingdom of Heaven!

During the time of St. Francis, there were two robbers who were causing havoc in the neighborhood. Once, when St. Francis was gone from camp, the two robbers showed up, and the disciples of St. Francis beat them and drove them away. When St. Francis returned, his disciples told him proudly, and with a sense of true achievement, of what they had done. Instead of being pleased with the news, St. Francis was sad. Tears came to his eyes, and he went to each of his disciples and begged forgiveness. He told the disciples that he had failed them, that had he taught them rightly about the love of God, they would not have acted in such a way. Instead of blows, they would have showered the love and understanding of God upon their enemies. Stunned, his disciples were humbled into silence.

St. Francis then sought out the two beaten and bruised

robbers and got down on his knees before them, begging their forgiveness. He told them what a failure he was, for not having taught his disciples how to show the love of God. Then he treated their wounds and fed them. The robbers were so impressed with this saint who was so poor in spirit, this little man who was so lacking in human pride, that they joined his band and became two of his most winsome and trusted disciples. In this instance, St. Francis *was* the Kingdom of Heaven, and that Kingdom was so attractive that the two robbers wanted it.

A personal story might illustrate this point further. I have stuttered since I was five or six years old. As a child, I dreamed that someday I might be able to speak in public. Many years have passed, and my dream has come true; I have spoken in public all over the United States, and in Mexico and Canada. I have discovered in these years that when I get myself into the picture and try to make a good impression, for the sake of my own pride, I have a difficult time speaking. Only when I lose myself in something else, only when I offer my body as a *living sacrifice unto God* for Him to do with as He wills, only when my mind is lost in Him, have I perfect ease and freedom in my speech.

Time after time I have faced a public-speaking situation feeling more nervous and inadequate than I could put into words, and time after time I have found the secret of "not being there." I have found the secret of emptying myself in order that God may have control of me. The emptiness becomes a fullness and a freedom when ego and pride are gone. One has to be willing to become a fool, if becoming a fool will enable God to have His way. It is true in public speaking, and in everything else.

Once I was speaking at a conference while a storm was

raging outside. Suddenly the lights went out. The room was plunged into darkness and my audience was blotted out. I could not even see myself. As I continued to speak, I became aware that I was not trying to make an impression on anyone. Thoughts and words flowed with a rapidity and a fluency which astonished me. It was as if I were standing off to one side and listening to myself. The secret was that I was "not there." In losing myself, I found a fluency and richness of ideas that was thrilling. Many told me later that it did not even sound like my voice.

Being completely poor in spirit is an experience we should always have, even while our eyes are open and we are aware of others. We should be so much "not there" that the Kingdom of Heaven within us would have perfect freedom to manifest itself in all our affairs.

Once I talked with a woman who had been under the care of a psychiatrist for some years. We were sitting on a hillside in New Mexico and my impression was that shock treatments and introspection had robbed her of all spontaneity. She seemed like a robot. Her speech and actions were rigid and mechanical. I tried my best to say something that might be helpful, yet nothing seemed to have any effect.

We sat there on a lovely mountainside, staring into the valley below. I had done all I could, and it was not enough. I waited, hoping that something might happen. For a long time we simply sat and stared into the distance, and I knew that if help was to come it would have to come from somewhere else.

Suddenly she gave a gasp. I turned and looked at her. She was staring incredulously at the surrounding scenery. She was enthralled by it. I was mystified.

"Oh," she said, "it's beautiful, it's beautiful!" Hungrily

her eyes drank in the scenery. Her breath came in short gasps. Color tinted her cheeks, and a sparkle, mixed with tears, showed in her eyes.

"What's beautiful?" I asked.

"Everything, *everything!*" she cried, and turning to me, she continued, "Yes, you are beautiful, too!"

She had come to me seeking help and had not found it, and in the depth of her disappointment, she had given up. But in giving up, she found all nature, all life, responding to her. Life had fallen into place. She had lost herself only to find herself, but it was her poorness of spirit that made it possible. Poorness of spirit had turned her into the Kingdom of Heaven, *related* her to the Kingdom of Heaven which is always here.

The poor in spirit react and respond to life from a center within themselves which is God. They respond to life as God responds to life. All separation is gone; in a sense, they are living in the Garden of Eden. They have vacated the seat of judgment, and given themselves wholly to the good, leaving whatever judgment there is to God.

When the scribe agreed with Jesus that the first and greatest commandment was: ". . . you shall love the Lord your God with all your heart, and with all your soul, and with all your mind, and with all your strength," and that the second was: ". . . love your neighbor as yourself," he was told, "You are not far from the Kingdom of God" (MARK 12:30, 31, 34).

It is not enough to be near the Kingdom of God. We have to embrace it as a way of living! The only way we can do this is to fall so much in love with God, to spend so much time with Him in prayer, that the enjoyment and the companionship of God is all that matters to us.

Dr. Harold Martin has a wonderful speech which he begins by saying, *"I have decided to live in the Kingdom!"* It takes a decision, and then it takes a commitment, the giving up of ourselves to that decision, in order to experience it.

"Blessed are the poor in spirit, for theirs is the kingdom of heaven"—theirs is the Kingdom of Heaven because *they are* the Kingdom of Heaven¹

2

Those Who Mourn

Blessed are those who mourn, for they shall be com-
*forted—*MATTHEW 5:4

WHEN we mourn we are not self-sufficient, or else
we would not be mourning. We have come up against
something hurtful that we are unable to handle. This is a
good condition in which to find ourselves, for then we are
compelled to reach out for something beyond ourselves.

If we were truly self-sufficient we would not need anyone
else, not even God. We would be a complete cosmos all to
ourselves. In fact, we would be unable to communicate with
others, for it is the incompleteness within us reaching out
to others for response that makes communication possible.

We need each other. Ultimately we need God—He who
ties all things together, even the entire cosmos of which we
are part, into perfect harmony and right relationship. Paul
says, ". . . above all . . . put on love, which binds everything
together in perfect harmony" (COLOSSIANS 3:14). John says,
". . . God is love" (1 JOHN 4:8). Only through God are we
able to bring ourselves and all things into right relationship.

Life is created in such a manner that it tends toward wholeness. Wound a tree, and the forces of life rally to heal it.

Break a bone, and the forces of life work toward healing the break. Lacerate the flesh, and immediately healing begins to take place. Burn a forest, and it is not too long before seedlings begin to sprout again and make another forest. All life tends toward wholeness.

To mourn, or to be sad, is not the natural state of God in man. And if it is not the natural state of God in man, or if it is not the intentional state in which God created man, then it is a wound or infection which all creation tends to obliterate—just as the white cells of the body, carrying out God's intention, gather at the point of infection to obliterate what is not normal in the natural creation of God.

Another proof that mourning is not natural is that we do not like to mourn. We dislike it. We rebel against it. We are in a state of unbalance, and yearn to get back into the balance of joy. God created us that way. If we had been created for sadness we would be "happy" in our sadness and want to continue in it. God has made us in His image, and when we are out of His image, our natures strive to return to the state of rest which is called joy. When we are in community with the nature of life, which, in this case, is joy and happiness, we are more useful to ourselves. We are of more service to others, we are creative, we are kind, we are generous, we are healthy. We more nearly and more completely reflect the image of God in which we are created.

The Apostle Paul says, "Blessed be the God and Father of our Lord Jesus Christ, the Father of mercies and God of all comfort, who comforts us in all our affliction, so that we may be able to comfort those who are in any affliction, with the comfort with which we ourselves are comforted by God" (II CORINTHIANS 1:3, 4). Note that Paul refers to God as the God of *all* comfort—not merely some comfort, but *all* comfort.

We sometimes think there are things in life which we simply could not endure. However, there are only so many things which can happen to us—the possibilities in this life are only so many. It takes little reading to see that there is nothing in life which we cannot find the strength either to overcome or to endure. Others have done it, and therefore the way is there for all to do it.

I was raised in a family of five boys, and when I was married I hoped that my wife and I might have a little girl. Well, my dreams and hopes came true. For eight years our lives with Mary Lou were all that could be imagined. Yes, there were high times and there were those low periods, but overall, having a girl in the family was all I had hoped.

Then one Saturday afternoon my wife Marion and I sat in a physician's office and heard him say that Mary Lou had but a few months to live. The shock was numbing. There had been no preparation for it. Mary Lou had been feeling tired, and sleeping a little overmuch, but no one had thought too much about it. The verdict was *leukemia*, with three months to live. Well, she lived for six months, and then died.

The hurt was *inexpressible*. One night during those last terrible six months, I was walking in the backyard alone in the darkness, trying to make some sort of sense out of the senseless—at least what seemed senseless to me. Because of a personal experience of years past, one of the foundation stones of my faith has been that either God is in all things, or He is not in any. Thus I believed that it was necessary to give thanks for all things. With this in mind, I breathed out something like: "Heavenly Father, I don't like this. I fail to see any good in it. Its hurts and seems a senseless waste of life and love . . . but for whatever way You are in it, I give You thanks."

Well, a miracle happened to me right then and there.

I had no idea how cold I had become. Suddenly I felt as if warm air were blowing through my body, as if great sheets of ice began to melt. And I knew that everything was all right. I did not know *how* it was all right. There was no hint that our little girl would recover. But something of the power and strength and comfort of God *dominated* me. The hurt vanished almost immediately and, I might add, "confusingly." I say "confusingly" because it still did not make sense to me that the fatal condition remained, that there was no evidence of Mary Lou's getting well, and yet in the face of this, I felt suddenly calm, and restored to normal actions and reactions. Yet it was true.

That feeling and awareness has never left me. I do not understand it, but I know that the power of God to strengthen and to comfort me then was more than equal to what I considered the worst that life could do to me. Those who mourn *are* comforted. The very vacuum which mourning creates draws to itself the relief and strength it needs. God made life that way because He Himself is that way.

A friend of mine once told me of a time of awful tragedy in her life. Her marriage had broken up and ended in a divorce. Beside herself with grief and confusion, she had driven all day in her car, not sure where she was going. She was simply going anywhere to get away. That night she registered in a motel, and alone in her room the backwash of months of repressed emotion swept over her. She wept as she had never done before. It seemed to her that her mind must snap. She would soon reach a point of no return. Then something happened. There cut through the storm of her uncontrollable emotion the words, "Be still and know that I am God."

The words (whether audible or inaudible, she does not know, but they had the effect of *audible words*) were spoken with a commanding tone she had never heard before, nor since. There was no possibility of disobeying them. In the midst of something horribly uncontrollable, peace swept over her. She knew she was not alone. She knew there was Someone capable and willing to make things right. That night she slept soundly, and wakened the next morning to a new world. She returned to her home, and since that time has led a life powered by an assurance that there is nothing God cannot handle perfectly.

The Psalmist knew what he was talking about, probably from personal experience, when he wrote: "Weeping may tarry for the night, but joy comes with the morning" (PSALM 30:5).

"Comfort" is not the same thing as "sympathy." The roots of the words have different meanings. Sympathy means "to feel with." *Pathos* means "feeling," "suffering," or "passion." *Sym* means "with." To be in sympathy with someone means to feel *with* him, to feel as he feels. If the other person feels crushed, you sense it and feel the same way. If someone is suffering the onslaught of fear, you are sensitive to it, and are suddenly afraid. It is a great gift to be able to do this. It approaches empathy, being at one with another. It is helpful in counseling, and in understanding someone else.

Once I was a speaker at a conference on Star Island, a lovely rock-bound island in the Atlantic Ocean off the coast of New Hampshire. There are sheer walls of rock there that rise out of the breaking sea, providing wonderful places to sit and look out over the water. One afternoon

I had seated myself on the rocks and was gazing toward the far horizon. It was a beautiful day. Sunshine bathed the world in lazy warmth, and I rested in a state of dreamy peace and perfect contentment. Then a very strange thing happened. A woman came and sat down beside me, and suddenly I became desperately afraid. My heart raced and seemed to leap into my throat. I was so afraid that I clutched the rocks beside me in order to steady myself. I was hoping that the lady would not notice how I felt. There was a pain in my left side, and the pins and needles of nervousness throughout my entire abdomen. The woman started talking to me about herself. The amazing thing is that as she described herself, she described exactly the symptoms I was experiencing. In some way, I had taken on her fears! I don't know how to account for this. Perhaps I had been in such a state of relaxation that the natural defenses of my ego were caught napping. There *are* such defenses which protect us from the undue influence of others. At least, this is the only way I can explain it. When I became aware of what I had experienced, I soon regained my self-control.

Something of the same thing can happen to each of us when we are genuinely in sympathy with another.

However, sympathy offers little help for the troubled person. It does him little good to have someone else roll alongside him in the mire and muck of human emotions. What he needs is strength to get out of his condition, to overcome the sorrow which is causing him hurt and harm. What he needs is to have his sadness turned into joy, his weakness turned into strength, his ignorance turned into wisdom, and his fear turned into confidence.

Comfort, on the other hand, offers more than sympathy. According to its Latin derivative it means "to strengthen much." It comes from two words: *con* (meaning "with") plus *fortis* (meaning "strong"). The God of all comfort is the God who is not only with us, but who also gives us strength to overcome the condition which has defeated us. Yes, God feels with us, knows our frame, our nature, and our hurt; but God also imparts to us the strength, the wisdom, the patience, and the faith to stand once more on our own feet, secure and strong.

A minister once told me that one of the things he says to those he visits in a hospital is this: "You can rest assured that God is on the side of your recovery." Then he reminds them that God has created life in such a manner that healing is the natural condition of life. Everything tends in the direction of healing. And why? Because in creating life out of Himself, in bringing into existence creation from Himself, God reflects His own nature.

God is perfect in all ways. His perfection is expressed in the laws and rules and principles of life. All these tend in the direction of perfection and wholeness. All things, when wounded, tend to heal. Therefore this minister tells his people: "Trust God in this matter of your recovery. Cooperate with Him through trust, and, by reminding yourself that He is in you, work out His perfect will."

The second beatitude finds its echo and reflection in all life. It is true that those who mourn shall be comforted. This is the way that life is made. When a man comes to the end of himself and reaches out into the darkness for something else, he finds there another hand which meets his and draws him up into a life greater than he had known before. He finds that in the darkness there is a light, in the weakness there is a strength, in the tears there is a joy, in the defeat there is a victory, in the indifference there is Someone who cares, and in the desolation there is a comfort.

Lee Nichols, confined to a wheelchair for years, once

wrote, "Loneliness is the silent hand of God reaching for the heart of man." Lee Nichols knew that those who mourn are comforted.

Perhaps this is the only way the Father of all life can teach us that we need Him, and that we need each other. Whatever the reason, all history and all life teach us that those who mourn shall be comforted. This is one of the great insights of human nature and a principle of existence. Happy is the man who early learns the secret of reaching out in his weakness and finding strength.

Those who mourn are in a place where God can visit them. Because of their distress, they are more easily led into the dwelling place of God. There they may experience the vision of St. John the Divine: " '. . . Behold, the dwelling of God is with men. He will dwell with them, and they shall be his people, and God himself will be with them; he will wipe away every tear from their eyes, and death shall be no more, neither shall there be mourning nor crying nor pain any more, for the former things have passed away' " (REVELA-TION 21:3, 4).

Jesus knew what He was talking about when He spoke the words of the beatitudes. He knew what life was all about. In His compassion and love, He taught it to us as clearly as possible.

> When peace like a river attendeth my way,
> When sorrows like sea-billows roll,
> Whatever my lot, Thou hast taught me to say,
> "It is well, it is well with my soul"
>
> H. G. Spafford

This lovely hymn was born in tragedy. Horatio Gates Spafford's wife and four little girls boarded the ship *Ville du Havre* for England, and in the middle of the Atlantic the ship was rammed by another ship. It sank within two hours. Mrs. Spafford was saved, but the four little girls were drowned.

Mr. Spafford had recently lost all he had in the great Chicago fire, and this new tragedy, on top of his business failure, seemed a crushing blow. He boarded a ship for England as quickly as possible to go to his wife. When he was in mid-Atlantic, the approximate spot where his children had drowned was pointed out to him. Weighted down under the burden of sorrow, he went down to his cabin and there wrote the words of this hymn.

In life's darkest hour, he had found the comfort of God because he knew the God of all comfort!

"Blessed are those who mourn, for they shall be comforted." This is the good news of the gospel.

3

The Meek

Blessed are the meek, for they shall inherit the earth
—MATTHEW 5:5

ANY interpretation of this beatitude must of necessity fit the facts of human history. According to the usual picture we have of someone who is called meek, he does not inherit the earth! Every theory must try to conform to the facts. Otherwise someone could say that it is a fact that the moon is made of green cheese, or that the planet earth is the center of the solar system. But scientific research does not validate such interpretations and theories, so we have discarded them and searched for others which more adequately explain and encompass the facts. Let us apply the same process of reasoning to this beatitude concerning the meek.

The beatitude implies that history bears out that the meek *inherit the earth*. If we assume that this beatitude is true, we must look at those who do "inherit the earth," or achieve in an outstanding manner, and see what the word "meek" implies.

There are two outstanding personalities in the Bible who are said to have been meek. One is Moses, and the other is Jesus.

Miriam and Aaron became jealous and angry with Moses—or perhaps they became angry with him because they were jealous of him. At any rate, they criticized him (spoke against him). ". . . and they said, 'Has the Lord indeed spoken only through Moses? Has he not spoken through us also?' And the Lord heard it. Now the man Moses was very meek, more than all men that were on the face of the earth" (NUMBERS 12:2, 3).

It seems quite out of character to describe Moses as "very meek, more than all men that were on the face of the earth." Moses hardly fit the common conception of someone who is meek.

Here was a man reared in a king's palace, a man who had a first-rate education, a man who was used to the good things of life, a man who was proud, a man used to having people obey him, a man with a violent temper, a man who had killed another in a fit of rage, a man who had fled from justice and had run a sheep ranch as a fugitive for forty years, a man who had returned to the country of his crime to face the king and his ministers, a man who had forced his will upon a nation, a man who had made his people journey toward Canaan against their wishes and wills, and a man who claimed he spoke for God! But here, too, was a man who had lost himself in a vision and a dream so completely that personal ambition ceased. The separated ego, which revolves only around itself, in a large measure no longer existed in Moses. He was so poor in spirit, or poor in *ego*, that it is questionable whether his ego influenced him at all in his highest and most intense moments of living.

Whether his poorness of spirit preceded his meekness, or the meekness (being lost in a purpose, dream and goal so big that it all but obliterates ego-centeredness) caused him to become poor in spirit, is unimportant. The fact is that his achievements were not due to personal ambition and willful pride, but rather to his having lost himself in something greater than himself.

Moses did inherit the earth. He inherited a nation. Because of his inheritance, multitudes of others were enabled to inherit the earth also.

Jesus was meek. He said so Himself. "Come to me, all who labor and are heavy-laden, and I will give you rest. Take my yoke upon you, and learn from me; for I am gentle and lowly in heart, and you will find rest for your souls. For my yoke is easy, and my burden is light" (MATTHEW 11:28-30).

Where the Revised Standard Version of the Bible reads "gentle," the King James Version reads "meek." I believe that the word "meek" contains within it more meaning than is generally attributed to the word "gentle." Jesus was gentle, but He was much more than gentle. He would permit no one, friend or enemy, family or stranger, to stand in the way of His goals and dedicated purpose. Quite evidently, meekness may include gentleness, but it also means more than gentleness.

Jesus was meek, yet here was a Man who identified Himself with a religious revolutionary (John the Baptist); a Man who disowned His own family and said that only those who did the will of His Father were His mother and brothers and sisters; a Man who faced up to the religious and political leaders of His day; a Man who claimed greater insight than the prophets of old; a Man who challenged people to lay down their lives for Him; a Man who declared that the Roman ruler of His land had no power over Him; a Man who said that no one could take His life from Him, but that He would lay it down of His own free will; and a Man who claimed that His words would never pass away!

The meekness of Jesus cannot be accounted for by personal drive nor by the inflation of the ego. He said that His will was to do the will of Him who sent Him. He had found a will greater than His own and lost Himself in it. He claimed that He had no power of His own, but said that it was the Father within Him who did the works. He claimed to have no words of His own, but said that it was God who spoke through Him. He acknowledged no goodness of His own, but said that only God was good.

Here, too, was a Man driven by a vision that the earth belonged to God, and that His own mission was to restore that relationship of harmony between God and man, and man and God. The vision on which He spent Himself was that earth could be heaven, and heaven could be earth. It was a fantastic dream, a dream that dwarfed personal ego into nothingness—and because of the nothingness, God the Father shone through Jesus. This was the secret of His power and attractiveness—His meekness!

Dag Hammarskjold says, in his book *Markings*, that his life was to spend and be spent. Here is the secret of achievement: it is to believe in something so deeply that the forces of one's personality are *lost* in it. Here, too, is the secret of denying oneself. Each of us has only so much energy. The more directions in which this energy is dissipated, the less there is available for each single direction. However, the fewer directions in which our energy is released, the more power will be exhibited in each one of them. If all our available energy is directed toward only one dominant purpose, the amount we are able to summon will seem miraculous in comparison to the little we could give to each one of a great many purposes.

Denying oneself means choosing to have one's life energies reserved for and directed toward a single goal, a single overpowering mission. A person with such a mission will seem to be possessed of miraculous energies and powers. In truth, he has denied himself the luxury of dissipation, and concentrated his energies on one selected purpose. When he thus loses himself, something far more worthy than self is born: he discovers the secret of meekness, the power of meekness, which inherits the earth.

Jesus demanded absolute loyalty and complete self-denial from those who would follow him. "Then Jesus told his disciples, 'If any man would come after me, let him deny himself and take up his cross and follow me. For whoever would save his life will lose it, and whoever loses his life for my sake will find it'" (MATTHEW 16:24, 25).

Again, "'He who loves father or mother more than me is not worthy of me; and he who loves son or daughter more than me is not worthy of me; and he who does not take his cross and follow me is not worthy of me. He who finds his life will lose it, and he who loses his life for my sake will find it'" (MATTHEW 10:37-39).

And, one more: "'He who loves his life loses it, and he who hates his life in this world will keep it for eternal life. If any one serves me, he must follow me . . .'" (JOHN 12:25, 26).

The world had better look out for a people who have become meek—poor in spirit, with a vision and loyalty that is more important to them than they are to themselves. Be careful of those who are willing to lay down their lives for what they believe and demand. On the other hand, "Where there is no vision, the people perish . . ." (PROVERBS 29:18, KJV).

The American Indian had courage, great courage, and yet he lost. He lost because he was not meek—he did not have a dream, a vision that was greater than himself. Had the Indian tribes been galvanized into action by a dream more lofty than the satisfaction of their own tribal comforts and needs, the white man probably would not have been able to subdue this continent. In the early days, especially, the Indians had enough warriors and weapons to drive the white man into the sea. In general, all the Indians wanted was to be left alone, each tribe in its own little domain. Without a vision bigger than that, they were doomed to failure.

The American Negro, however, perhaps because of the efficiency of mass communication in our times, does have a dream, a dream for which he is willing to lay down his life. Here is the main ingredient of the power of meekness.

We have always thought of the Negro as being poor in spirit. Until recent times he had to be; he had no choice in the matter. He was a slave, at first legally, and later socially and economically. But, whatever caused it to come about, a dream and a vision and a demand gradually began to crystallize and take shape. With the formation of the dream, meekness began to be exhibited.

The Negro's hope of success is that meekness will not degenerate into mere brashness and human bravado. If it does, he will lose. If he continues in meekness, the achievement of his goal will be inevitable. It will take discipline on his part; it will take responsibility on his part; and, it will take sacrifice on his part. The legal guarantees of equal opportunity are only a beginning. The Negro will also have to educate himself so that he can take advantage of the opportunities which exist.

Assuring legal protection and providing opportunities does not automatically guarantee that people will make use of these advantages. There are millions of white people in the

United States who have all the legal opportunities and possibilities for achievement, but they are still living in poverty and ignorance. The legal assurance of opportunity is necessary, but if it is not put to good use, if the dream is lost, all the laws in the world are not going to enhance the position of the Negro in the United States, or, indeed, anywhere else.

The dream is all-important. Losing one's self in something greater than one's own estimate of his worth is more important than all the human effort involved, and than all the laws ever framed.

Scholars have said that there is no English word which adequately interprets the meaning of the original Greek word which has been translated as "meekness." The closest we can come is in two words of French derivation: "debonair" and "nonchalant." These two words taken together give an entirely different idea of meekness. They connote something that is far from the widely-held idea of a weak-willed doormat who is easily frightened away from his purpose.

It is not enough to *appear* debonair and nonchalant. It is easy to put on a false front, to be a hypocrite. The appearance must be the result of something that genuinely motivates us. Ultimately, this something has to be the dream of God—a vision and a purpose so overwhelming that it engulfs us, and we are completely lost within it. The result will be that we will find a new freedom, a new release, and a new courage that we never dreamed was possible.

Others may mistake the outward symptoms and say that *we* are unusually gifted and courageous. The opposite is the case. The reason for such achievements is not personal ambition; rather it is that we are so completely "not there" that the Kingdom of Heaven within us has the freedom to release in us all the possibilities for attractive behavior that lie dormant in each of us.

The history of "inheriting the earth" is the history of the meek. Artists have starved and left their families because they were captivated by a dream beyond their power to deny. Their meekness of spirit, because prideful ego was not involved—or so slightly involved by ordinary social standards —enabled them to become channels for something greater than themselves. They starved, they were rejected by society, they were condemned, they were beaten and jailed, but art was all that mattered to them.

This does not mean that all of us should do the same thing. Dr. Harold Martin said to one young man who was considering the ministry, "If you can get along without the ministry, don't go into it; if, on the other hand, you can't live without the ministry, go into it." The same rule must have applied to artists who achieved and inherited the earth, even if the recognition of that inheritance came long after they were dead.

Actors who have achieved, and have inherited the earth, in general, paid for their achievement by suffering poverty and hunger along the way. They chose to act, even badly in the beginning, rather than to be fairly comfortable doing something else. Acting was their life. Acting was their goal. Acting was their vision. Acting was bigger than they were. Because of this "something bigger" in which they lost themselves, they found a courage and a release which finally catapulted them into success. Meekness was the answer.

In business, too, meekness is the key to achievement, to inheriting the earth. A man I knew was the janitor of a small college. A few students helped him produce a wax for floors, and with their help he began to produce it in his garage.

The time came when the manufacture and distribution of wax became his chief goal. For years he made very little money out of it; in fact, he poured what little money he had into it. He poured his dreams, his talent, his time, and his energy into it, too. Many a night he went without sleep so that his salesmen would have enough wax to sell the next day. It took years during which He gradually added more and more products to his line, but finally distributors all over the country began to carry them. He was a success. One day he was even successful enough to buy out the industrial vacuum cleaner subsidiary of a giant company.

Yes, this man did, in his own way, inherit the earth. But it came about only after he had given himself to a dream and lost himself in it. In losing himself he found himself, and in finding himself he found power and wisdom and courage that he did not realize was available to him.

Someone has said that the best way to get ahead in life is to go into debt—a strange thing to say, but with some truth in it. A debt can act as a stimulus which concentrates one's time and energies. The desperation of not wanting to fail will tap powers and energies beyond one's normal capacity. This too is meekness.

One of the meekest men I ever met was Dr. B. P. Hivale of India. He had been a professor of philosophy at Wilson College in Bombay for twenty-two years, and seemed settled for life. Recognition and economic security were his. Then he became captivated by a dream.

He had come from a very poor section of India, and the memory of the destitution of its people kept returning to haunt him. The time came when he knew that he wanted to start a college there, in order that the area might be improved, and the people—his people—might experience the fullness of life he had come to know. Although he was married and had a family, Dr. Hivale resigned and gave himself to the great dream. Ahmednagar College was founded, and today has over twenty-five hundred students.

This little man traveled all over the earth to find money for his school. Wherever he was, personal acceptance or rejection mattered little to him. Insurmountable problems did not defeat him. Personal defeat or success was not capable of making him deviate from the vision. Some of us used to play a little game. We would change the subject and try to see how long we could keep Dr. Hivale off the topic of his college. No one ever succeeded for long. He always managed to bring the conversation back to center.

Some people might say that Dr. Hivale had great courage and drive and ambition. They would be wrong. It was because he had none of these things, at least in the usual meaning of the words, that he succeeded.

In a real sense he "was used" by something which so far exceeded himself that the forces, powers, principles, laws, and energies of life found a channel to express themselves in human terms. The power, the motive, and the goal were ultimately God's, but God's work could only be done because Dr. Hivale was meek.

A child standing before a television set, engrossed in watching a performer on the screen, automatically begins to imitate the expressions and characteristics. The child has forgotten himself; he has lost the little shyness and embarrassment of the ego. He has become meek.

Meekness is the secret of greatness, the secret of inheriting the earth. This meaning of the beatitude is the one which is in harmony with the facts of human experience. It is true that the meek do inherit the earth. Nothing stands in their way. They are so much "not there" that God shines through them with clarity.

The beatitude implies that God Himself is meek, and so He is. He causes the rain to fall on the good and the evil, and the sun to shine upon the just and the unjust; and the attributes of His nature, such as love and justice, are neither conditioned nor changed by our acceptance or rejection of them. God is the same yesterday, today, and forever—regardless of what we may think; II Timothy 2:13 puts it this way: ". . . if we are faithless, he remains faithful—for he cannot deny himself."

Blessed are the meek. All history proves that they *do* inherit the earth.

4

Those Who Hunger and Thirst

Blessed are those who hunger and thirst for righteous-
*ness, for they shall be satisfied—*MATTHEW 5:6

THE text of this beatitude quite evidently is not referring
to physical hunger and thirst. It says, ". . . they who hunger
and thirst *for righteousness*. . . ." It is referring to those who
are attracted to certain thoughts, ideals, and dedications.
However, the allusion to hungering and thirsting, both physical sensations, is quite appropriate. There comes a time in
everybody's life when the physical necessities and comforts
are not enough. There has to be a way of living and a set
of standards which make even the most luxurious physical
satisfactions palatable.

The reason is that man is not primarily a physical being,
but rather a spirit. In the final analysis of the human situation,
it is only the things of the spirit, of the mind, and of the
will, which can give man the sense of interior rest and satisfaction. One who is held prisoner in the most luxurious surroundings still knows that he is a prisoner, and wants to
escape. Things of the mind and the spirit are primal to everything else.

It has been said that if one wants security, the best place

to find it is in prison. In prison a man does not even have to think. The activities of his whole day are planned for him. All he has to do is fit in with them. If he wishes even to acquire a college education in prison, it is possible for him to do so. Here is security in the extreme. Yet who willingly would take advantage of it? No, there is something forever free in the human breast, something which hungers and thirsts after meaning, after pattern, and after that elusive element which makes life worth living.

A man can die from hungering and thirsting after mental and spiritual things, just as he can die from hungering and thirsting after material things. It is probably true that most of the suicides in the world are not committed by those who are physically hungering and thirsting, but rather by those who have the material benefits of life yet have been unable to find a reason for going on. Yes, hungering and thirsting, spiritually and mentally, can kill you just as effectively as hungering and thirsting after bread and water.

There are many references in the Bible to hungering, thirsting, and desiring. One of the chief reasons why people respond to the Bible as they do is because it recognizes human nature for what it is. Implicit in the entire Biblical account is the belief that man's nature and propensities are God-made; and when used as God intended them to be used, they result in strength and blessing.

Jesus recognized the power of desiring. Mark 11:24 records: "Therefore I say unto you, What things soever ye desire, when ye pray, believe that ye receive them, and ye shall have them" (KJV). He might just as well have said that whatsoever things we hunger and thirst after, when we pray. . . . It would have meant the same thing.

There is tremendous power in simply hungering and thirsting, whether it be in the material realm or in the spiritual one. If a man wants a thing badly enough, he will usually get it. I believe it was Emerson who said that we are praying all the time, and that unfortunately our prayers are being answered. By this he meant that we are continuously and constantly expending time and energy and talents, and that our reward is usually just those objects or intentions upon which we expend them.

Once Jesus said, "Ask, and it will be given you; seek, and you will find; knock, and it will be opened to you. For everyone who asks receives, and he who seeks finds, and to him who knocks it will be opened" (MATTHEW 7:7, 8).

Someone who is well versed in Greek has said that this passage should read: ". . . everyone who asks *and continues to ask* . . . seeks *and continues to seek* . . . knocks *and continues to knock*. . . ." It is not the expression of some transitory whim that Jesus is referring to here, but of a deep-seated and deep-rooted goal, a desire which will not be thwarted by temporary defeats and delays. This kind of asking and seeking and knocking becomes a way of life, something that a person is hungering and thirsting for, down to the very depths of his soul, and those who live this way find the doors of life opening to them.

However, Jesus' statement about asking and seeking and knocking is another indication of His recognition that desire, or hunger and thirst, is of great benefit and power to anyone who experiences it. Hungering and thirsting generates an emotional intensity which becomes the driving force toward achieving desired ends. An individual who does not have great desires and dreams to impel him is like a wave driven by the sea. He becomes a pawn of every circumstance, and a plaything of every situation. The man who is indifferent is letting his energies go to waste.

Our desires, our hungerings and thirstings, do not always

seem rational to the outward view. This does not mean that they are irrational, however. The very fact that we are attracted by something, or want something, is evidence that whatever it is we want has awakened a response within us, even if that response is unconscious.

C. T. Studd said that whenever God wanted to tell him anything, He first put a desire into his heart. Such a desire may make little sense to us at the time we become aware of it, but subsequent experience will always show that there was nothing haphazard about the desire and its results.

Many writers and speakers have said that we should give our dream to God, but not tell Him how to bring it to pass. What they are actually saying is that the methods and means by which dreams, hungerings and thirstings, come true are beyond the scope of our present knowledge. When we try to specify the methods and the means by which we think they ought to come true, we are often making it impossible for them to happen. The events that we think might be reasonable and efficient could in reality be the very ones which would prevent our dream from coming to realization.

As an example, take the mailing of a letter. We may pour our hopes and dreams and yearnings into a letter, but the destination of that letter, the means by which it reaches its goal, has to be placed in other hands. Someone has said that if we take a letter to the mailbox we have to let go of it in faith and in trust. Then the machinery of the United States government will see that it reaches its destination. As long as we continue to hold on to one tiny corner of that letter, it can go no place. However, if in the trust which we have in our government, represented by the tiny stamp we have placed on the letter, we let go of the letter and drop it into the mailbox, the resources of a multi-million-dollar organization called the Government of the United States can go to work for us. Our letting go of the letter is like the little seed of faith which Jesus talked about in the Gospels.

Similarly, we must take our hungerings and thirstings, our desires and our yearnings, to God, and in trust leave them there. We can give God the finished picture of what we want, dream into it with all the emotional content that we can muster, but we can not tell God how to do it. We must trust Him enough to know that He knows the best way.

I was at a conference in the eastern part of the United States when one of the boys who was attending was arrested by the police in a nearby town. This boy had previously been released from the custody of the court in his hometown in order to attend a conference of this sort. On the day of his arrest, he and a few other boys had driven into town and parked their cars there. His hometown court had ordered that this young man was not supposed to get behind the wheel, and in fact he did not drive any of the cars into town. However, after the cars were parked, he and another boy were asked by a resident of the town to move their car and thus make it easier for the resident to get his own car out of the cramped parking area. The second boy did not know how to drive, so our boy decided that he would move the car a little in order to help the stranger. When he started up, something went wrong and his car rammed into the car in front of it. The police came, and he was taken to the police station. A telephone call was made to our camp at just about prayer time that afternoon.

On that particular day I had charge of the youth prayer group. They were crushed by the information that this young man, who had come to camp seeking help, was now in the hands of the police. I told them to close their eyes and imagine the most perfect thing that could happen in these circumstances. I told them to picture it as clearly in their minds as they possibly could, to feel it as intensely as possible. After they had done this, I asked them to tell me their thoughts and their feelings.

One said that he had imagined the police chief to be a father himself, and very understanding. Someone else said that he could picture the individual whose car was damaged realizing that this could happen to anybody, and that while the boy may have been foolish, there was no intent to do harm. Another said that he could see the young man himself not becoming bitter and giving in to defeat, but instead, having a loving and outgoing attitude to those who were involved in the whole situation. All in all, they painted, quite specifically, as ideal a solution to the problem as could be imagined.

Then I said something like this: "This is the best we can think of with our human minds. It makes sense. What we have thought and felt is good. Now let us take all these pictures we have imagined, and all these feelings which we have experienced, and in simple, childlike trust give them into the hands of God. He is the great Architect of life, and only He knows how to bring the desires of our hearts to fruition."

The remarkable thing about this story is that what these young people had desired and imagined came true just about one hundred percent. When the young man in trouble returned from town with his friends, we had the awesome feeling that they had been listening in to the things we had said in the prayer group. Almost item by item, their description of what had happened matched what we had asked in prayer, believing, with simple childlike trust.

There are many things which could be said about this

experience, but the thing I want to emphasize is that in addition to desiring we also have to have trust. And this trust ultimately has to be in God.

There is power, great power, in hungering and desiring, but unless we hunger and desire *after the right things* (righteousness) we are not going to be too happy with the results. Those who achieve greatly in life are those who are powered and motivated by great drives, by great dreams, by great hungerings and thirstings, and by great goals and ambitions. They are driven on by the emotional content and clarity of their goals and ends. The sad thing is, that many who spend years of time and energy and talent and emotion achieving their goal are disappointed when they get it. In not hungering and thirsting after the right things (righteousness), they are dissatisfied. They continually find it imperative to seek a new goal in order to forget the bittersweet of a victory that was in reality a failure.

What would happen if all your dreams came true? What do you want out of life? Just suppose that everything upon which you are spending your time and your energy and your money and your emotions *happened to you right now.* Would you be satisfied?

Not all people come to God, or reach out for something beyond themselves, because they have failed. Many do it because they have succeeded too well. When their dreams have come true—when they have all the money they want, all the recognition and reputation they desire, when they finally live in the surroundings they have always dreamed about, have married the one they wanted, and so on and so on—they find no satisfaction in them. Then they reach out for God.

It does us all good to sit down every so often and delineate our goals to ourselves. What do we want out of life? What do we wish to be? What kind of personality are we striving to achieve? What has meaning for us? Where do we sense that we came from and where do we desire to go? What values do we have which are not dependent upon the passing scene? What is eternal and what is temporal, and how do the two merge? When we are old and able to look back on our lives, what will we be proud of? What will we be ashamed of? How do all these questions relate to the jobs we now hold, to the lives we are now living, and to the world of which we are a part?

Probably none of us will ever come to specific and perfectly clear answers about any of these basic questions of existence. However, there is a tendency in every man's life which is beyond himself. We know it is good. It wants to contribute to the benefit and well-being of mankind. It yearns for the One who is involved in, and who is in back of and in front of, this thing we call life. We demand God and His righteousness in order to be satisfied.

Hunger and thirst, yes, but hunger and thirst after the right things, because whatever you hunger and thirst for is what life will give you. Unless life offers us rest for the soul and satisfaction for the mind, there is little reason for going on. Nothing is more beautiful than to see these who have lived close to God for a great many years, resting and satisfied in their old age. There is beautiful repose in their manner. There is a cleanness and a clearness about them. There is a tenderness and a trust in their behavior and actions. They have harvested the fruit of years of companionship with Someone who is infinitely beautiful and strong—God.

These people remind one of the story of Ernst and the

Great Stone Face. Some day, so legend promised, there would return to the little town in the shadow of the Great Stone Face a native son who had gone out into the world and achieved greatness, and he would have the profile of the Great Stone Face in the mountains. Over the long years many had gone from the town and achieved greatly in many areas—military service, the ministry, and so forth. Whenever one of these native sons would return, the whole village would gather to see if he looked like the Great Stone Face, and year after year they were disappointed. Then one day someone happened to be passing by the little home of Ernst, a simple man who lived in the shadow of the Great Stone Face. Ernst had gone out day after day, throughout his entire life, and stood and gazed up at the mountain. Who knew the things he had shared with it?—the tears, laughter, births, deaths, disappointments, frustrations, joys, festivities?—in fact the very fabric of his life? As the passer-by looked at Ernst, suddenly he realized that it was Ernst who looked like the Great Stone Face—strong, craggy, dependable, a very mountain of rest and strength.

The Psalmist says: "One thing have I asked of the Lord, that will I seek after; that I may dwell in the house of the Lord all the days of my life, to behold the beauty of the Lord, and to inquire in his temple" (PSALM 27:4). Perhaps it takes years of all sorts of experience, both good and bad, to come to the final realization that the only thing we can truly hunger and thirst after is God. If we hunger and thirst after Him, if we seek after Him, if we ask after Him, and if we knock at the portals of life after Him, we shall surely find Him. We shall find Him in everything in which we are involved, everywhere, in the very breath that we breathe, and thus we shall find satisfaction. "As a hart longs for flowing streams, so longs my soul for thee, O God" (PSALM 42:1).

One whose life is God-centered and God-directed—because he desires it to be so, because he hungers and thirsts after it—will automatically find himself involved in the right things of life. He will enter into the right relationships of life, whether he is a school teacher, a bus driver, an airplane pilot, a gas station attendant, a hardware store clerk, or whatever. In the framework of his own personal relationships he will find that which is good, and he will give himself to it in effort, talent, and ambition. In the process, he will find satisfaction.

Yes, blessed are those who hunger and thirst for righteousness, for they will find satisfaction.

5

The Merciful

Blessed are the merciful, for they shall obtain mercy
—MATTHEW 5:7

MERCIFULNESS means unmerited goodness and unearned generosity. Jesus expressed it this way: "But I say to you that hear, Love your enemies, do good to those who hate you, bless those who curse you, pray for those who abuse you. To him who strikes you on the cheek, offer the other also; and from him who takes away your cloak do not withhold your coat as well. Give to every one who begs from you; and of him who takes away your goods, do not ask them again. And as you wish that men would do to you, do so to them" (LUKE 6:27-31).

Jesus continues: "But love your enemies, and do good, and lend, expecting nothing in return; and your reward will be great, and you will be sons of the Most High; for he is kind to the ungrateful and the selfish. Be merciful, even as your Father is merciful" (LUKE 6:35, 36).

Implicit in these passages is the attitude that life lived fully and rightly must reflect the nature of God. Jesus says that we ought to do these things in order that we may be sons of God, or sons of the Most High. If God is the Creator and the Sustainer of all life, if the laws and principles of the universe are expressions of the nature of God, then in order to come into right relationship with life we must express the nature of God.

To be merciful (generous without limit) is to be like God. It is the result of coming into right relationship with Him. It is evidenced by coming into harmony with all creation, because all creation is the expression of God Himself.

Life is merciful. It is unearned and unmerited. We do not have to go back and recreate the great masterpieces of literature; they are handed to us freely. We do not have to recreate the great paintings of the world; no, they are all there for our enjoyment. We have at our fingertips the results of millions of years of human striving and achievement. We do not have to rediscover the laws of science which make life so comfortable for us today; no, they are given freely for our use and benefit. Life is extravagant and generous and free. It is merciful.

Most of our friendships and pleasures are unmerited and unearned. Oh, we may say that we earned them, but when we look at ourselves and others more objectively we find that much—in fact, most—of what we have, we had little to do with obtaining. No friendship ever lasts if those involved in it feel that they are obligated to each other. Friendship, like love, is a spontaneous outgoingness of nature that is unmerited, and cannot be repaid except with a similar spontaneous outgiving of oneself.

Scripture tells us that God has not judged us according to our iniquities, but rather has shown mercy; He has removed our transgressions from us as far as the East is from the West. God is merciful because it is His nature to be so. It is the way He is!

This truth is reflected in all of life. The nature of electricity is not compromised nor conditioned by our use or misuse of it. It continues to be true to itself, and to operate according to its own laws.

God, the very Essence of life, is true to His own nature. He is the same yesterday, today, and forever—eternal, unchanging, and dependable. If this were not true, the universe as we know it would be impossible.

If there is one thing upon which all our knowledge is based, it is that truth repeats itself. Once we discover something, it may be verified by anyone, at any time, under the same circumstances. A person's religion, color, nationality, traditions, social status, or economic position have nothing to do with his perception of truth. Truth is universal.

Hence, the primitive idea that God is conditioned by our reactions finds no echo in anything else we know about life. The mercy of God—that is, the generosity of the nature of God—is unchangeable, always there, true to itself, or as the Psalmist said a long time ago, His mercy "is renewed every morning" (PSALM 90:5).

Like God, and in harmony with the laws of nature, are those who are merciful—that is, profligate in their goodness. Does this agree with what we know about life? Does it agree with that which is behind life and therefore expressed in the laws of nature and of all living?

Fish in the ocean spawn their eggs with an abandon and a generosity that is astounding. How many millions of possibilities of life are deposited into the waters is beyond measure. The answer is in the billions of billions. It is true that only a small percentage of these possibilities come to life, for many reasons, but the generosity and the necessity for that generosity is nonetheless constant. The same thing is true of the propagating habits of most insects. Again, one may say it is a practical necessity that this happens, but that does not negate the richness of the sowing of the seed and the bringing forth of teeming armies of offspring. Nature is determined that some will live and perpetuate the species. And the same may be said for human life. Millions of sperm are released in order to make sure that conception takes place, and this superabundance of life material is proof of nature's determination that fruitfulness will occur.

The beatitude gives us an insight into abundant living. One of the prime laws of living is that like produces like. This secret ought to be etched on the determination of every youth, and illuminated in the memory of every adult. *Like produces like! As we sow, so shall we reap!* If we sow poverty—materially, mentally, emotionally—we shall reap poverty. If we sow mercifully, that is, abundantly and generously, we shall reap in like manner. The poverty-stricken personality receives from others in like measure. One who withholds from others finds that others withhold from him, while one who gives of himself to others finds that others give to him.

Glenn Clark, when he was a college professor, demonstrated this to his students. At social gatherings for freshmen he always sought out the young men and women who were ill-at-ease. He would tell them that he had selected them to help other students who were having a difficult time adjusting to the social life of the evening. Pointing out three or four others who were standing off to one side, he would urge the shy students to see that their awkward colleagues entered into the festivities of the evening. He would suggest asking them to dance, inviting them over to the table for something to eat, or talking about where they were from and what their family was like. Before long, the shy students were so busy making others feel at ease that they were having a wonderful time, too.

In being generous with his time and talent, a shy student found that he had gained many friends and acquaintances. His own generosity and mercifulness had returned quickly to bless him with the same seeds he himself had sown.

In order to take full advantage of the laws of electricity we have to place ourselves in harmony with those laws, so that they can cooperate with us, and their powers and secrets can be of use to us. We not only have to learn something of its nature, but we also have to have wiring and generators to enable electricity to flow to us. Similarly, we can place ourselves in harmony with life's laws and principles. We can receive more fully and readily the kindness of others when we ourselves are kind. We shut off and prevent most of the kindness of life when we ourselves are unkind.

Remember the great law of this beatitude—*like attracts like!* This is why Jesus said to give and it would be given to you, to love even the ungrateful and it would be returned to you. This is, once again, the law of sowing and reaping. If we sow sparingly, we shall reap sparingly. If we sow bountifully, we shall reap bountifully.

The soil of life gives back to us according to the seed we plant. If we plant weeds, we will get weeds in return. If we plant corn, we will get corn in return. Everything returns to us according to its own kind. Everything! Sow the seeds of bitterness, and bitterness will return to you. Sow the seeds of indifference, and you will reap a harvest of indifference. Sow the seeds of generosity, and life will return generosity to you in like manner. Sow the seeds of love and goodwill, and the time will come when the soil of life will reward you with what you have sowed, only multiplied. " . . . put me to the test, says the Lord of hosts, if I will not open the windows of heaven for you and pour down for you an overflowing blessing" (MALACHI 3:10). "Judge not, and you will not be judged; condemn not, and you will not be condemned; forgive, and you will be forgiven; give, and it will be given to you; good measure, pressed down, shaken together, running over, will be put into your lap. For the measure you give will be the measure you get back" (LUKE 6:37, 38).

Do not trim the sail of your life according to the behavior of others. Set the course of your own life. Do not blame your failure on the winds of adversity. The same wind will drive a sailing ship west, and it will also drive it east; it all depends upon the set of the sail! So it is with your life. Be merciful, generous as a way of living, just as your Father in heaven is generous.

To be merciful is to expend one's self in excess of the needs and demands of the situation. It is not like the law of an eye for an eye and a tooth for a tooth, which is but a refinement of unbridled destruction. At least the law limited a person bent on vengeance from doing anything in excess of the damage done to him: he could not kill a man because he had had a tooth knocked out; the most he could do was to take a tooth in return from his opponent.

But this law has nothing whatsoever to do with mercy. Just as unbridled savagery is on the side of destruction, mercy is on the side of goodness. Mercy consists of returning good for evil, helping your enemy, doing good to those who despitefully use you, and praying for those who persecute you.

Mercy is generosity carried to the extreme. It knows no limits. Mercy bears within itself its own impetus. It is not conditioned by its reception. It spreads itself broadcast, without stint. If you sow generously of your time, talents, and interests, they will return to you in generous achievements and rewards—*good measure, pressed down, running over, will be yours.*

I went to college with a student named Willard Peterson, who had to work his way. For a year we both were janitors in a local church. Willard had one knack that seemed perfectly natural to him, although I am sure he had to learn it, like everyone else does. Whatever he gave himself to, he gave himself wholeheartedly. He was interested in everyone and in almost everything, and he threw himself into things with abandonment. He wanted to be a physician, and he studied toward that end as generously as he did everything else. While many students did only enough work to get by, Willard was always doing an extra amount of work in the laboratory, or at his books. His curiosity was insatiable. It is little wonder that he did excellent work in medical school, and later became a medical specialist. Yes, life has paid him back generously in reputation, economic rewards, and status in his profession. He deserved it. But Willard Peterson got in like measure what he had given all along the line.

The principle of life is that he who expends himself generously will be generously rewarded. "I will sing of mercy and judgment: unto thee, O Lord, will I sing" (PSALM 101:1, KJV).

Judgment without mercy results in retribution, and nothing more than that. Retribution does nothing to prevent a crime from taking place again. In fact, it often makes it more likely that a crime will be perpetrated. Many times a first offender is sent to jail, only to find himself among hardened criminals. In such an environment of hate and confirmed criminality, he is infected with the same disease as the other inmates—unsociability, desire for vengeance, and disrespect for law and order. The result is the confirmation of a man's criminal tendencies, when a little mercy would have paid dividends in his future regard for law and order.

Today much of our penal system does not deal in retribution, or at least the more enlightened courts do not deal in it. As far as possible, retribution is tempered with mercy. More and more, people are given understanding and a second chance. And, where possible, first offenders, if they are sent to prison, are separated from habitual offenders. Even in the tough business of crime and punishment we recognize that mercy must accompany judgment if the result is to be the good of all.

Tom, a youth I know, rebelled against the divorce of his parents, with nearly disastrous results. Until the time of the separation of his parents, Tom had led a rather normal life. He was a good student in school, and participated in all the activities of a normal teen-ager. After the divorce, it was not long before he stole a car. He was caught, and placed on probation. This seemed to have no effect for good at all. In a short time, he had stolen another car. This time he was sent to a boys' town under the jurisdiction of the courts. He ran away, and again he was caught. He was given psychiatric treatment this time, and then placed in a foster home. After some time he was returned to his mother's home. In the last few years, Tom seems to have readjusted his life to normal patterns. He plans to enter college soon. The heartache of past years has been replaced with hope for the future.

One shudders to think what would have happened to

Tom if the courts had not been understanding and hopeful. Some people said at the time that the courts were too lenient, but how much better for them to have been lenient than to have veered in the opposite direction! This young man has been saved not only for himself, but for all society. In the years to come, society will be paid back for its mercy many times over by having prevented tragedy and heartache. Yes, the Psalmist was right; he was right to sing about judgment *and* mercy.

Jesus was the incarnation of mercy. Jesus was generous beyond the call of duty with His time and talents. In spite of sufficient cause for resentment against the scribes and Pharisees, He took time out of a busy schedule to talk with Nicodemus by night. He spent himself on the multitudes, and taught His disciples to do the same, so much so that they had no time even to eat. After Peter denied Him, Jesus still treated him with understanding and kindness. When two other disciples misunderstood His intention and mission in life—even after walking with Him and being taught by Him for three years—and they wanted positions of power in an earthly regime, Jesus was patient and kind in His explanation and treatment of them. He had time for the individual in the midst of the crowd—the blind man, the crippled woman, and so many others. Even when He was suffering the agonies of death on the cross, He had the mercy and generosity to comfort a dying thief by His side.

Not many a man in history has spent himself so freely, even to the voluntary giving of his own life, as did Jesus. But the judgment of history is that probably no other man has received so generously the love and self-givingness of mankind.

The merciful do receive mercy. It is a law of life. It is

the way the universe is built. It reflects the very nature of God himself.

"Blessed are the merciful, for they shall obtain mercy." This is the great secret of abundant living and achievement. It is not simply an idealistic religious precept. It is not limited to any one aspect of living. It is not some dreamy hope. Rather, it embraces the all-ness of living. *It is the way of life itself.*

6

The Pure in Heart

Blessed are the pure in heart, for they shall see God
—MATTHEW 5:8

IN the mind of Jesus, the pure in heart are those who live solely unto God, whose behavior is determined by their dedication to God, and whose motive in life is to express the nature of God. The pure in heart are the single-minded. They sense all things as coming from God, and recognize that all life is an expression of God.

The entire sixth chapter of Matthew is concerned exclusively with this type of God-centered living. With typical insight and practical analysis, Jesus recognizes that rewards are the common denominator of human effort. We do whatever we are doing for some utilitarian reason. We want others to know what we are doing, we want to be commended for it, or to be paid for it in some way. Perhaps we are seeking the security of achievement and acceptance.

Jesus tells us that we do things either to be "seen of men" or to be "seen of God." In either case we get our reward. Our only choice is: Whom do we want to reward us? For instance, Jesus mentions the giving of alms, fasting, and prayer.

If we do these things to be seen of men, we will get our reward. People will be impressed. They will undoubtedly say, "What a good man he is! There is a truly spiritual man, a godly man." They might even contribute to our causes and missions!

But Jesus warns us not to be the kind of people who think, or act as though they believe, that recognition and security depend upon the good will of others. He tells us to pray, to give alms, and to fast *unto the Father*, and that the Father who sees in secret will reward us openly. In fact, He indicates that we should keep private our religious practices so that men will not be apt to reward us because of them. Jesus goes on to say that in the basic motives of living, no man can serve two masters. He will be loyal to one and not to the other, or he will hate one and love the other. Then He capped this passage with "You cannot serve God and mammon" (LUKE 16:13).

Then is recorded one of the most loved and attractive passages in the entire Bible, as Jesus continues: "Therefore I tell you, do not be anxious about your life, what you shall eat or what you shall drink, nor about your body, what you shall put on. Is not life more than food, and the body more than clothing? Look at the birds of the air: they neither sow nor reap nor gather into barns, and yet your heavenly Father feeds them. Are you not of more value than they? And which of you by being anxious can add one cubit to his span of life? And why are you anxious about clothing? Consider the lilies of the field, how they grow; they neither toil nor spin; yet I tell you, even Solomon in all his glory was not arrayed like one of these. But if God so clothes the grass of the field, which today is alive and tomorrow is thrown into the oven, will he not much more clothe you,

O men of little faith? Therefore do not be anxious, saying, 'What shall we eat?' or 'What shall we drink?' or 'What shall we wear?' For the Gentiles seek all these things; and your heavenly Father knows that you need them all. But seek first his kingdom and his righteousness, and all these things shall be yours as well" (MATTHEW 6:25-33).

The purity of Jesus' single-mindedness, His abandonment to one dedication and one will, is shown clearly in the above passage, with its counsel to seek first the Kingdom of God and His righteousness. Jesus does not discount the importance of the things of life, the material benefits and needs, but He says that basic to all of these and underlying them all is a right relationship with God. He reminds us that God is just as provident in the affairs of men as He is in the affairs of the lilies of the field.

The question that each one of us must answer is, "Whom am I really trusting?" To him who is pure in heart there is only one answer: "God." We can trust our own intelligence and our wits to gain us the securities of life, but if the material benefits are all we get, if there is no overall commitment and sense of direction, the getting of the material benefits is not worth the struggle. After getting them, many have committed suicide.

He who is pure in heart does not miss the material benefits of creation. He needs them as much as anyone else; but in entering into the spirit which lies behind all materiality, and which brought it into being, he finds that materiality is his as well. If this were not true, then one would have to come to the conclusion that creation and God are entirely separated and separate, and that whatever kind of a "sub-god" keeps creation functioning must be in competition with the God who is over all. This becomes a ridiculous argument, and has to be discarded. God is the God of *all*. "This is My Father's world," and He has provided for us.

Living exclusively under God may seem impractical in our modern world, but is it really? If one believes, or knows, that being in harmony and alignment with God is expressed spontaneously in right relationship with all creation, this will naturally include relationships with people and all the conditions of life. If we can come into community with the very spirit and essence of life itself, we will naturally and easily be in community with the individual elements of which life is composed.

A man who knows that one of the great rules of all life is service will naturally be of service wherever he is. He is not going to have his actions determined by the particular person with whom he happens to be at the moment. If his attention is on the particular person, and he is judging whether or not it is worth his efforts to spend himself in some sort of service, he may guess wrongly. Later on he might find out that the one he did not think was capable of rewarding him and his efforts was the very one who could have done the most for him. On the other hand, the person who is living unto God is not going to make this mistake. Service to others will be his natural propensity. Because his life and the life of God will have merged with each other in the mystery of commitment, he will not be able to keep himself from broadcasting the seeds of service everywhere.

So it will go with all the other attributes of God expressed in human terms. The man who makes them a part of his life will be loving in his relationships, he will be honest in his dealings with everyone, he will be a source of joy and happiness wherever he is, he will instill confidence and faith everywhere, and he will infect others with peace.

"Pure" means to be unadulterated, to be unmixed with something else, to be single, to be unconfused. The pure in heart are those who realize that all life is an expression of God, and therefore all life is to be held in awe and reverence. This is the basis of the life and philosophy of Albert Schweitzer—*reverence for life*. If all things were created by God, and without Him was nothing made that was made, and all things created are in existence this moment by the continuing indwellingness of God in every atom, then as we serve things we are serving God. This is the reason why Jesus said that if we brought our gift to the altar and there remembered we had anything against our brother, we should leave our gift on the altar and go and first be reconciled to our brother. The pure in heart see the oneness of all creation. They see that materiality is, in truth, but one expression of the Body of God Himself.

In the twenty-fifth chapter of Matthew, Jesus tells a story of the final judgment: "Then the King will say to those at his right hand, 'Come, O blessed of my Father, inherit the kingdom prepared for you from the foundation of the world; for I was hungry and you gave me food, I was thirsty and you gave me drink, I was a stranger and you welcomed me, I was naked and you clothed me, I was sick and you visited me, I was in prison and you came to me.' Then the righteous will answer him, 'Lord, when did we see thee hungry and feed thee, or thirsty and give thee drink? And when did we see thee a stranger and welcome thee, or naked and clothe thee? And when did we see thee sick or in prison and visit thee?' And the King will answer them, 'Truly, I say to you, as you did it to one of the least of these my brethren, you did it to me.' Then he will say to those at his left hand, 'Depart from me, you cursed, into the eternal fire prepared for the devil and his angels; for I was hungry and you gave me no food, I was thirsty and you gave me no drink, I was a stranger and you did not welcome me, naked and you did not clothe me, sick and in prison and you did not visit me.' Then they also will answer, 'Lord, when did we see thee hungry or thirsty or a stranger or naked or sick or in prison, and did not minister to thee?' Then he will answer them, 'Truly, I say to you, as you did it not to one of the least of these, you did it not to me'" (MATTHEW 25:34-45).

Jesus did not say that it was "as if" they had done it unto Him, but that they *actually had done it to Him!* When one becomes so single-minded and rooted in God that he recognizes all of life as the literal expression of God, then whatever he does to anyone, to any single item of creation, is actually done to God Himself. Jesus was so at one with God, and God had so completely manifested His own nature in Jesus, that it does become true that what we do to others we are doing to Jesus. We are doing it to Jesus because Jesus is at one-ness with the eternal Father.

The pure in heart, those who are exclusively God-centered, those whose wills and emotions and thoughts are God-aligned, do see God in every flower, in every tree, in every person, in every breath they breathe, in everything their eyes fall upon. God is all. There is no separation in life. They are in community with God, and with the expression of Him in human terms, knowing that in some mysterious manner they and the Father are one.

Now we come to the second part of this beatitude, that the pure in heart shall "see God." We are so used to associating "seeing" with physical eyesight that we often forget that "seeing" is accomplished in many other ways.

It is quite common that, when someone explains something to us—perhaps something in arithmetic which may have mystified us—and we suddenly come to understand it, we exclaim, "Oh, now I *see* it!" What we really mean is that now we understand, or mentally perceive, it. It is not something that we actually see with the eyes, but rather with the mind. Perhaps we could say that we see it with the eye *of* the mind. In the same way, when someone is telling a story we will often interject, "I see, I see." We do not mean that we are seeing something with our eyes, but rather that we are following the thread of the story with our understanding.

If we include all the meanings of the word "see," in our understanding of it, then we certainly "see" as much with our minds as we do with our eyes. In fact, we could say that we see even more with our minds and understanding than we do with our eyes, for the outer eyesight is actually dependent upon the inner understanding or perceiving. It is doubtful if we could see at all (even if our eyes were in perfect physical condition) if our minds were so feeble as to be incapable of identifying or being aware. So, in the truest sense of the word, seeing is the understanding of the mind.

Blind people have other ways of seeing. They "see" by sound and by touch. A blind person can tell by the sound of his cane how near he is to the edge of the sidewalk. He can tell by the difference in temperature if he has gone from the sunlight into the shade. I am told that there is even an awareness of some sort when a blind person approaches a large object, such as a building.

And there are other things a blind person sees because he is not dependent on physical sight. Helen Keller tells us that she can tell, or "see," the mental or temperamental condition of people who come into the room she is in—whether they are courageous or afraid, happy or sad, trusting or suspicious. By the feel of their hands she can "see" something of the personality of the people she is meeting.

Like the man in the Gospel story who was blind and regained his sight, we too can say about many things, ". . . one thing I know, that, whereas I was blind, now I see" (JOHN 9:25, KJV). In regard to knowledge—how blind we were about the human body before we studied anatomy! How blind we were about the electric toaster before we had to fix the plug! How blind we were about the capacity to learn before we took a course in psychology! In fact, how blind we were about literally millions of things of which we had had no experience!

The art of seeing is actually the art of collecting and collating and identifying data, and then of organizing it into meaningful wholes. Two people may look at the same set of facts, or view the same scene, and come to entirely different conclusions. There is the story about two men walking out into the night: one saw mud and the other saw stars. What you see depends upon what you are looking for. This is why Jesus admonished His listeners to seek first the Kingdom of God and His righteousness. We usually find what we are looking for.

There is a legendary story about Jesus which points the moral that it is possible to find something good in anything. It is said that there were some people who had never heard Jesus say anything unkind about anyone. This seems hardly possible when we recall some of His remarks about the scribes and the Pharisees. Nevertheless, according to the story, these people were determined to find something that would make Him react in anger or revulsion. One day when

Jesus was walking along the road with them, they came upon a dead dog. The animal had been dead for some time, and in that hot region it was not a pretty sight. They deliberately stopped and pointed it out to Jesus, and waited to see what He would do. After a while He turned to them and remarked, "What white teeth he had!"

There is some truth about the nature and personality of Jesus in this legend. He found things to commend that others were blind to in people—like the women taken in adultery, the women who spilled the costly ointment on His head, the publicans, the sinners, and foreigners such as the Gentile centurion.

It is said that to the pure all things are pure. This is true. It does not mean that the beholder always sees the pure being used in a pure manner, nor in the right way. It means that one who is filled with Spirit, one who is seeing everything through the eyes of God, recognizes every act as good in itself and potentially a blessing, providing it is used as God intended it to be used.

After a person comes into right realization of God, and right relationship with Him, he still continues to eat and sleep and expend his energies. However, now they are expended in directions which are of benefit and service to all mankind, whereas before the same energies were being expended in wastefulness and hurtfulness. The one who is pure sees the saint in every sinner, the beautiful in every ugliness, the success resident in every failure, the joy in every sadness, and the worth in the unworthy. He sees life through the eyes of God, and sees the image of God in everything and in everyone.

There is a story about a king of an ancient kingdom who chose a good man and a bad man from among his people.

To the good man he said, "Go out into the kingdom and find an evil man." The good man searched and searched, but he could find none. To the bad man the king said, "Go out into the kingdom and find a good man." The bad man, too, searched and searched, but he could find none. Thus, to the pure all things are pure. To the evil all things are evil. We see life through the eyes of our own inner man!

The pure in heart *do* see God. They see Him in every person, they see Him in every event, they see Him in every tree, in every mountain, in every ray of sunshine, in the air they breathe, and in the circumstances of living. They see Him in the seasons of the year: the color of the autumn foliage, the bareness of winter, the stirring of spring, and the fullness of summer. They see God everywhere, because they understand that all life is directed and sustained, moment by moment, by the spirit which is God. Call it what you will, it makes no difference—Spirit, Energy, Mind, Father, Flux— anything you wish. But always the understanding is that behind the phenomena lies the invisible which gives it existence. A poet once said that God is aflame in every bush, if we have but eyes to see it.

William H. Carruth, in his poem "Each in His Own Time," expresses the same thought:

> A fire-mist and a planet,
>   A crystal and a cell.
> A jelly-fish and a saurian,
>   And caves where the cave men dwell;
> Then a sense of law and beauty
>   And a face turned from the clod—
> Some call it Evolution,
>   And others call it God.

A haze on the far horizon,
　　The infinite, tender sky,
The ripe, rich tint of the cornfields,
　　And the wild geese sailing high—
And all over upland and lowland
　　The charm of the golden-rod—
Some of us call it Autumn,
　　And others call it God.

Like tides on a crescent sea-beach,
　　When the moon is new and thin,
Into our hearts high yearnings
　　Come welling and surging in—
Come from the mystic ocean,
　　Whose rim no foot has trod—
Some of us call it Longing,
　　And others call it God.

A picket frozen on duty,
　　A mother starved for her brood,
Socrates drinking the hemlock,
　　And Jesus on the rood;
And millions who, humble and nameless,
　　The straight, hard pathway plod—
Some call it Consecration,
　　And others call it God.

In the fourteenth chapter of John we find an incident which throws light on Jesus' attitude concerning the seeing of God. "Philip said to him, 'Lord, show us the Father, and we shall be satisfied.' Jesus said to him, 'Have I been with you so long, and yet you do not know me, Philip? He who has seen me has seen the Father; how can you say, 'Show us the Father?' Do you not believe that I am in the Father and the Father in me? The words that I say to you I do not speak on my own authority; but the Father who dwells in me does his works. Believe me that I am in the Father and Father in me; or else believe me for the sake of the works themselves' " (JOHN 14:8-11).

Philip might well have reacted in shock and answered, "How can a man be God?" But if he had said this, he would have been looking at a physical body without realizing the One who was behind and in that body. He would have been looking at the outside and forgetting the supremacy of the Spirit which inhabited that body. He would have been looking upon a man as separate from the Source of life, instead of "seeing" with his understanding the Spirit which made Jesus what He was.

In the high-priestly prayer of Jesus, in the seventeenth chapter of John, He petitions the Father that . . . "they may be one even as we are one, I in them and thou in me, that they may become perfectly one . . . (JOHN 17:22, 23). Such a relationship comes about through the pure acceptance of our relationship with God. It comes through obedience and dedication to the will of the Father expressed in all human relationships. This is sonship. It is the experience of the Psalmist: "I will tell of the decree of the Lord: He said to me, 'You are my son, today I have begotten you' " (PSALM 2:7).

In this relationship of "seeing," all life becomes holy. We "see" and understand that life continues to exist only because of the life and Spirit of God expressed in every atom. The pure in heart, the dedicated, the single-minded, the holy abandoned, do see God.

Blessed are the pure in heart, for they shall see God!

7

The Peacemakers

Blessed are the peacemakers, for they shall be called sons of God—MATTHEW 5:9

A child embodies the nature of his parents. A child of God displays the nature of his Sire.

It would be natural for one who knows his sonship—his true heritage of being made in the image and likeness of God—to do the things that God does, to behave as God behaves—as a peacemaker.

There is a legend that during the time of the Crusades, St. Francis walked across the battlelines and met with the ruler of the Moslems. He talked with him about the love of God, and what God had done in Francis' own life. When he was through speaking, the ruler of the Moslems said something like this: "If your armies came in your spirit, there would be no war." If they indeed had, there would have been what Dr. Frank Laubach is calling for today—*"a war of amazing love"*! Can you imagine an army of St. Francises? It would not take a very big army of that sort to conquer the world!

A peacemaker has a holy calling. Whether he moderates labor disputes between government departments, or among neighbors in international crises, a peacemaker is truly the ambassador of God. He receives from God wisdom and power beyond himself, because his work is in community with God and His nature.

If to be blessed is to come into community with God, then the beatitude must mean that God Himself is a Peacemaker. Of course God is a Peacemaker, for whenever anyone comes into harmony with Him, he is endued and endowed with peace.

When Elijah fled from Queen Jezebel, he finally stopped in a cave. The story is recorded in the nineteenth chapter of I Kings, verses 9 through 13: "And there he came to a cave, and lodged there; and behold, the word of the Lord came to him, and he said to him, 'What are you doing here, Elijah?' He said, 'I have been very jealous for the Lord, the God of hosts; for the people of Israel have forsaken thy covenant, thrown down thy altars, and slain thy prophets with the sword; and I, even I only, am left; and they seek my life, to take it away.' And he said, 'Go forth, and stand upon the mount before the Lord.' And behold, the Lord passed by, and a great and strong wind rent the mountains, and broke in pieces the rocks before the Lord, but the Lord was not in the wind; and after the wind an earthquake, but the Lord was not in the earthquake; and after the earthquake a fire, but the Lord was not in the fire; and after the fire a still small voice. And when Elijah heard it, he wrapped his face in his mantle and went out and stood at the entrance of the cave. . . ."

The peace, the quietness and stillness, was evidence that God had visited the prophet, or perhaps that Elijah had become so still that he was able to be aware of the God who was always there. One of the gifts of God is peace. God is a peacemaker, and those in community with Him are peacemakers, because God releases in them His own nature.

Peace is basically a spiritual commodity. It embraces the domain of the body, the realms of the mind, and the sweep of the emotions. Physical relaxation is but another way of describing physical trust. One relaxes in a chair only if he has perfect trust that the chair will bear his weight safely. Relaxation, in the physical sense, is the evidence (the outward and visible symptom) of interior trust.

Serenity is the evidence of mental trust. It is the outward and visible sign that a person's analysis of himself and his situation is *in* good hands. He has nothing to be anxious about. Calmness is the outward and visible sign that he is emotionally secure and has no need to be afraid.

Peace, however, includes the mental, the emotional, and the physical. Spiritual trust—knowing that the ultimate and eternal purposes of life (the beginnings and the ends) are beneficent and dependable—suffuses the mind and the emotions and the body with the peace that passes understanding.

Glenn Clark often used to say, after he had prayed for someone, "I know that prayer is right—I have such a feeling of peace about it." A prayer that ends with one still in a state of fear, anxiety, and confusion is evidence that he has not given the problem (or himself) into the hands of God, into the trust of God. There is still doubt in his mind, either that God has not heard, or that He is perhaps unable or unwilling to hear. Such a person is still trusting only in himself.

When we place money in a bank, we leave it there and go about our business, confident that it will be taken care of. Our trust oftentimes is manifested by a sigh of relief, by calming of the emotions, and by mental rest; whatever we have entrusted is in good hands. A "trust fund" is something we believe will be kept safe and secure for the future. Real prayer is based on a kind of trust, and it also manifests the same results.

The Apostle Paul tells us in just a few words the perfect method of prayer, the perfect attitude toward life, and the perfect result, in Philippians 4:4-7: "Rejoice in the Lord always; again I will say, Rejoice. Let all men know your forbearance. The Lord is at hand. Have no anxiety about anything, but in everything by prayer and supplication with thanksgiving let your requests be made known to God. And the peace of God, which passes all understanding, will keep your hearts and your minds in Christ Jesus."

When we have truly put ourselves into the trustworthy hands of God, it is cause for rejoicing. And it results in peace. The solution to our problems may still be veiled from our eyes. Even though we do not know how things are going to work out, peace reigns within—a peace which comes through trust in the goodness of God.

Peace (and the making of peace) is the art of restoring things which are out of proper relationship back to the intention of God (perfect balance). Things in perfect balance are not in a state of stress and strain. There is a rest. The Psalmist said it: "Return, O my soul, to your rest; for the Lord has dealt bountifully with you" (PSALM 116:7).

When Jesus walked on the water to meet His disciples, and they cried out in fear, He said, "Fear not, it is I." When He got into the boat, it is said that the storm died down and calmness reigned. So often in the personal storms of life, men and women have found the same thing happening inside their souls after they reach out and invite Him into their lives.

A friend of mine was preaching along Skid Row in Los Angeles, and a young woman was listening to him. She evidently had led a dissolute life, but she was hanging onto his every word. When he finished, she told him that she wanted help. He had the urge simply to say to her, "Stand where I was standing, and say the words, 'Jesus, Jesus, Jesus.' "

Trembling, she walked to the spot he had pointed out, as the crowd watched. A long struggle took place within her. Perspiration wet her face. Time after time she opened her mouth to speak, but no sound came forth. Gently my friend urged her to say the words, and the time came when she uttered, "Jesus, Jesus, Jesus." Then she took a deep breath. Relaxation and peace settled over her, and she stopped trembling. A look of childlike gratitude came over her face. She turned to my friend and said, "Oh, I feel so good, so good, calm. I can't remember when I felt this way. It's real." She had taken Jesus into her life and had found the peace of God. Like God, Jesus is a Peacemaker, because He is in community with God.

Often we become so enmeshed in the many demands of living, and the many problems, that we have to retreat from them to gain a new perspective. One Saturday afternoon I was downtown in Estes Park, Colorado. The streets were jammed, and it seemed to take forever to get a few errands done. I was in a hurry, but the more I tried to rush about, the less I was able to accomplish. The crowds moved at a certain pace, and there was not much anyone could do about it. Irritated and frustrated, I finally finished my errands and left for the countryside.

Later that afternoon I sat on the side of a mighty mountain and saw, away in the distance, the town of Estes Park. How small it looked from there! How insignificant seemed the problems that had plagued me earlier in the afternoon. In the quietness and greatness of the mountains my world had fallen into place. Peace reigned. "Be still, and know that I am God" (PSALM 46:10). To gain peace within ourselves it is often necessary simply to stop doing whatever it is we are doing—to be still. This is why it is a good idea to force ourselves sometimes to break the cycle of activities that are reducing us to nervous exhaustion.

Do something else! If you can find a retreat of silence, all the better. It is amazing what stillness will do for the mind. If the stillness can last for a number of days, the time will come when a deep, bone-settling peace will envelop you. If silence is enforced to the extent that only limited amount of visiting is permitted, you will become aware of an Otherness and your relationship to it. You will see yourself and your circumstances more clearly. In the new perspective, you will find a peace you hardly knew before.

Jesus said, "Peace I leave with you; my peace I give to you; not as the world gives do I give to you. Let not your hearts be troubled, neither let them be afraid" (JOHN 14:27). Peace is, therefore, one of the attributes of a life in community with God. It ought not to be a transitory peace, a little temporary oasis of calm in a welter of anxiety, but a permanent peace which is not dependent upon circumstances. It is truly the "peace that passes all understanding."

A friend of mine, after visiting a man soon to be electrocuted, remarked: "He had more joy and peace than I had, who was supposed to help him. He helped *me*. I knew by looking at him—and talking with him—that he was completely in the hands of God."

I sat beside the bed of a beloved friend, who was ill with cancer and not far from death. I found no hint of anxiety or fear or apprehension; there was a peace and calmness about her that, from every human viewpoint, did not make sense. Yet it was real. She said to me, "We think we know so much, and we know so little. God is real and you have nothing to fear." Disease had had its way without hindrance, and yet there was no doubt that, having had its way, it had lost the battle. The body it might destroy, but this spirit was triumphant. The evidence of God was the peace, the sureness of perfect calmness, never wavering. She looked death in the face, smiled, and went to her Father, who was greater than she.

This friend was the perfect illustration of what it says in Psalms 4:8: "In peace I will both lie down and sleep; for thou alone, O Lord, makest me dwell in safety."

In Isaiah 26:3 it says: "Thou dost keep him in perfect peace, whose mind is stayed on thee, because he trusts in thee."

Peace is the result of trust. Without trust there can be no peace, only anxiety. Ultimately this trust has to be in God. Perhaps we have to learn from a whole series of little trusts to come finally to the big trust in the Overall-ness of life. However it comes, trust is the answer.

It is not enough to have one's mind "stayed" on God. Many whose minds are stayed on God are in mental institutions. They are completely obsessed with the conception of God, but the conception they are obsessed with is that of a Being of fear and vengeance. They do not *trust* God—they *fear* Him. And, according to their conception of God, they ought to fear Him. Their God is not infinitely greater and kinder than man, but rather infinitely more brutal and despotic.

The God we are talking about is the God revealed by Jesus of Nazareth, the One He taught us to call "our Father."

Jesus' conception of God is rich with such descriptions as "kind," "generous," forgiving," "provident," "abundant," "life-giving," "patient," and "understanding." Here indeed are attributes of a Being we can trust. Here is a Personality so attractive that we voluntarily reach out to Him.

There is another thing that ought to be said about the role of a peacemaker. It is difficult, if not impossible, to be a peacemaker if one does not have *peace within himself*. Jesus did not tell us merely to be at peace; He said that He gave, and would give us, *his* peace. He had peace to give! So the first thing that a peacemaker has to do is to find peace within himself; then he is able to pass it along to others.

A friend of mine told me that whenever he has what appears to be a particularly distressing and difficult day ahead, he gets up an hour earlier in the morning in order to "enter the silence." In the silence he reminds himself of the omnipotence, omniscience, and omnipresence of God. He reminds himself that he belongs to God. By an act of his will, and by the desire of his heart, he gives himself completely into the hands of God. He reminds himself of the might and the power of God. He reminds himself that there is nothing that God cannot do. He remembers that with God all things are possible. He remembers that with God nothing shall be impossible. He tries to clear his mind of all anxiety and doubt and, in a childlike manner, place himself mentally into the sea of trust which belongs to God.

Oftentimes he will call to mind some incident in the Bible. One of his favorite passages is the story of the disciples who locked themselves in an upper room because of fear. According to everything they knew, Jesus was dead. Their dreams and hopes had been dashed. But Jesus came through the walls of fear and breathed "peace" on them.

Then my friend imagines that the same thing is happening to his affairs, and to himself. He imagines the breath of God breathing peace into what seem to be troubled circumstances, calming the waves of human confusion. As he envisions a scene such as this, he tells me, a calm sweeps over his mind and body and soul, and he knows that he is in the care of God who made heaven and earth. He has nothing to fear.

Then he might remind himself of the words of Jesus—that the time would come when His disciples would be forced before kings and princes "for his sake," but that they should not be anxious! When they were supposed to speak, the right thoughts, ideas, behavior would come to mind and they would act in a manner that would prove the wisdom of God.

My friend tells me that many times his mind has become so panicked by fear that only in meditation and silence can peace be restored. Facts and figures which had eluded him suddenly come back to him. And he testifies that this comes about only through trust in God, and, that his life is in God's hands.

In James 3:18 it says: "And the harvest of righteousness is sown in peace by those who make peace." The harvest of righteousness is the abundance and evidence of our right relationships with each other, with the universe, and with God. James says that the seed of this is sown not in striving and stress and anxiety, but in stillness and in peace! And it is sown by *those who make peace.*

The peacemakers, those who *make* peace because they *have* peace within themselves—*these are the sons of God.* Like God, revealers of God, expressions of the nature of God —such are the peacemakers, for they are the offspring of God.

8

Those Who Are Persecuted for Righteousness' Sake

Blessed are those who are persecuted for righteous-ness' sake, for theirs is the kingdom of heaven

—MATTHEW 5:10

IF heaven is the full and uninhibited expression of righteous-ness, then those involved in, and working for, the cause of righteousness on earth represent the Kingdom of Heaven. In a sense they are in heaven here on earth, doing what comes naturally. Righteousness, or right relationships in all things, is the climate they breathe. It is their way of life, and they are committed to the belief that righteousness is the intent of God for all mankind. Their mission is to restore man to his sacred and holy inheritance in God.

Our laws are constantly being reformed to protect the rights of individuals. A belief in the sacredness of the human personality is at the root of these efforts. Our system of government is committed to securing protection and equal rights for the individual. This commitment, too, stems from our belief in the sacredness of the human personality.

Our courts have decreed that everyone has the right of attorney, regardless of how poor he might be. Once again, it is our reverence for human life which calls forth such decisions. Our police force can only secure evidence by well-defined rules and laws. For example, they may not enter a person's home without a legal search warrant. This is quite different from what we know happens in Russia and China, where the individual is viewed from an entirely different standpoint.

To be committed to the way of righteousness is to be in conformity with God Himself, according to Jesus and the Hebrew prophets. The way of right relationships—dignity, justice, understanding, liberty—is the expression of God in human affairs. Those who work to achieve such ends are vehicles through which God expresses Himself. They reveal the dreams, visions, instincts, and demands which God has created in man. They work to change and improve social systems which violate God's nature in man. They work to usher in "the acceptable year of the Lord."

In all cultures and in all periods of history there have been those who risked their own safety and popularity to challenge man to a more just and kind way of life. These stood above the expediency of the moment to say, "Thus saith the Lord. . . ."

When King David used intrigue to take another man's wife, Nathan the Prophet would not let even a king escape judgment for such a deed. In the time of Isaiah the religious system was challenged to practice its precepts when the prophet told them that the "fast of God" meant feeding the hungry, clothing the naked, and refraining from gossip and the pointing of an accusing finger. The tribal customs of Abraham's time came face to face with it when the patriarch learned it was not right in the sight of God to sacrifice human life. The Church of Rome came up against it when Luther posted his ninety-five theses on the door of the church at Wittenburg. Public executions, which used to be occasions for picnics, are things of the past because "prophets" stung the conscience of our western nations with "Thus saith the Lord. . . ."

In all ages and areas, those committed to the righteous God have been persecuted because they have been and are the Kingdom of Heaven in their own time. When one decides to battle the enemy, he must count the cost, and yet forge ahead, by faith. The Lord said to the Prophet Jeremiah: "They will fight against you; but they shall not prevail against you, for I am with you, says the Lord, to deliver you" (JEREMIAH 1:19). And fight they did against one of the greatest prophets who ever lived.

"Now Pashhur the priest, the son of Immer, who was chief officer in the house of the Lord, heard Jeremiah prophesying these things. Then Pashhur beat Jeremiah the prophet, and put him in the stocks that were in the upper Benjamin Gate of the house of the Lord. On the morrow, when Pashhur released Jeremiah from the stocks, Jeremiah said to him, 'The Lord does not call your name Pashhur, but Terror on every side. For thus says the Lord: Behold, I will make you a terror to yourself and to all your friends. They shall fall by the sword of their enemies while you look on . . .'" (JEREMIAH 20:1-4).

Jeremiah was *involved* in the cause of righteousness, and it brought him persecution! Those who are willing to endure persecution for the cause of righteousness must be completely committed. This commitment must be more than mere mental assent; it must mean involvement—in the case of Jeremiah, to the extent of being beaten and put in stocks!

A friend of mine who is a clergyman knows what it is to be persecuted for righteousness' sake. This story about him, which I was told by a mutual acquaintance, sounds like fiction, but it is true. My friend was pastor of a church in a western state, and he spoke out against the gambling syndicate there, and made himself very unpopular with those who said that gambling was good, that it brought in money and business to the community. Where there is gambling, there are also fellow travelers, such as prostitution, and my friend's town was no exception. Girls were imported for prostitution purposes, and the babies born were sold through some sort of an adoption "racket." It was quite a complex and involved system and many people were caught up in it.

The minister was threatened, in person and by phone calls. His wife and children were threatened. A bomb was thrown at his home, and because of it he was deaf for some time, but later recovered his hearing. Gradually, public opinion rallied around him, men who believed in his cause sought and succeeded in attaining public office, and the syndicate had to move out.

The only reason that this man and his family could endure such extreme pressure was that he was totally committed to the cause of righteousness. Living in any other manner was inconceivable to him. The Kingdom of Heaven was his homeland, and he lived to extend its borders.

One would not be persecuted "for righteousness' sake" unless he were attempting to change the contemporary system. Obviously such a person is not in harmony with the present social, political, and moral systems. Obviously, also, he is in community with another system of living which goes under the name of the "way of the righteous." Such a person is evidently "in" the Kingdom of Heaven, in mind, dedication, spirit, and will. He is already living it, therefore he is out of sympathy and loyalty with society as it is.

The Scriptures tell us "not to be conformed" to this world, but rather to be transformed by the renewing of our mind in Christ Jesus. Not to be conformed to the world by definition means that one will be "out of whack" with it, and be compelled to bend all his energies to transforming it according to the goals and ideals to which he has given his life.

The goal of "for righteousness' sake" is the full and free expression of the will of God in creation. When limited to human affairs, it means for the sake of right relations in human affairs—justice, charity, opportunity, freedom, liberty, economic security, dignity, health, peace, all the attributes of God in human terms. The beatitude implies that there is a divine plan and holy pattern for human living which is available now. It also implies that our present society and our lives are in need of changing.

Change never comes easily, in any age. All systems of men and government contain entrenched interests which will battle to maintain the status quo.

Those in positions of influence are not readily going to let go of the reins of power. There will be all sorts of traditions to affirm that the present system is just and adequate; those who want to change it will be exposed to strife and hostility. No matter how right they are, and no matter how history may vindicate their decision, persecution and ridicule must be their lot. The fact that they are on the side of righteousness does not shield them from persecution.

Now, persecution is not to be sought after for its own sake. Some people have made this very mistake. They assume that because they are having a difficult time, this proves they are in community and communion with God. Such people are apt to quote, "In the world ye shall have tribulation . . . ," but persecution and righteousness are not always related.

Criminals believe they are being persecuted when the police prevent them from carrying out their designs. It is common for those in prison to feel that society has persecuted them, regardless of what they themselves have done to society. The dope peddler feels persecuted by the authorities. A lazy and dissolute man feels persecuted when he is fired from his job. Yet, by every standard of normal living, these "persecutions" are necessary and just. Jesus only commends persecution for the sake of righteousness: only such persecution shows that the person who suffers it is in alignment with God's great design for human living.

Commitment to the way of righteousness must never be identified with any particular social system. The way of righteousness applies to them all, in all times of history. If one is committed to justice, the application of it is the same in our present system as it was in the times of the Hebrew prophets. It was wrong for a merchant to give short change, or short weight, in the time of Isaiah, and he spoke out against it, held it to the light of judgment, and worked to eradicate it. It is equally wrong, by the standards of our own political and social systems, to be unjust, and to give short change in any way today. It is against the law, and many "prophets" in business and government have worked to enact such laws.

Because of the efforts of those involved in righteousness in our time, we have child labor laws, fair employment practices acts, and fair housing laws. Just as the prophets of old were persecuted "for righteousness sake," these prophets of our own age have been persecuted "for righteousness sake." Change does not come easily.

Those who led the struggle for women's suffrage were held up to ridicule, some were beaten, and many were jailed. They knew what it meant to be persecuted. But they did it because they were committed in their hearts and minds to justice. Justice will always be one of the expressions of the way of the righteous. People will always be committed to the way of righteousness, for God planted it in the human heart. People will always be impelled to work for changes that make life more nearly reflect the holy design of God for man.

Mahatma Gandhi was a man committed and involved in the cause of righteousness. While he was still a young man in Africa, he was refused permission to join a Christian church because he was an Indian. Yet this young man had fed on the words of Jesus, and wished to join the cause and embrace the Spirit of Jesus. If he could not do it officially, as a member of the Christian church, he would do it in the Spirit of Jesus. And so he did. There came a time when the little brown-skinned man led the millions of India. He marched to the sea and protested against the salt tax. He was thrown in prison, and spent years there during the course of his lifetime. In the beginning he was laughed at and ridiculed. How dare this little, insignificant creature think he could bring the British Empire to its knees! *Yet, he did!* His mission and his work is an example of "Not by might, nor by power, but by my Spirit, says the Lord of hosts" (ZECHARIAH 4:6).

The cause of righteousness has always been advocated and fought for by those who believed that God's divine plan entailed reforming the systems of man. Many gave their lives for it, but eventually the spirit of righteousness in mankind responded to them, and change took place.

We would be wrong if we assumed that such changes only take place through the efforts of religious people. Religion has often been on the side of maintaining the status quo, economically, politically, and socially. What we are talking about is that *something*, the dream and the vision which God the Creator has placed in the hearts of all men everywhere. It is that something, created in the image and likeness of God Himself, which makes man strive for liberty, justice, and all other ideal standards which he attempts to attain when the Kingdom is in his own heart. We are talking about the human necessity to reach for something lofty and beautiful, a need placed in man's heart by the Creator.

To the one who rests in God, who finds his joy in the things of the Spirit, there is a home-ness and a contentment that is not dependent upon the well-wishers of society. There is a strength in righteousness that feeds the soul, and blesses the one committed to it with a peace and sureness that mystifies the world. Paul said it so well: "I know how to be abased, and I know how to abound; in any and all circumstances I have learned the secret of facing plenty and hunger, abundance and want. I can do all things in him who strengthens me" (PHILIPPIANS 4:12-13).

And who is this One who strengthens you? *God Himself!* "He is the source of your life in Christ Jesus, whom God made our wisdom, our righteousness and sanctification and redemption; therefore, as it is written, 'Let him who boasts, boast of the Lord'" (I CORINTHIANS 1:30).

The one who is engaged in the cause of righteousness is able to continue his work because he is "hid in the life of God," and feeds upon Him. Being fed and hid there, he is already in the Kingdom of Heaven.

Blessed are those who are persecuted for righteousness' sake, because they are the expressions of the Kingdom of Heaven, they manifest it in human form; ". . . theirs is the kingdom of heaven."

9

The Reviled and Persecuted

Blessed are you when men revile you and persecute you and utter all kinds of evil against you falsely on my account. Rejoice and be glad, for your reward is great in heaven, for so men persecuted the prophets who were before you—MATTHEW 5:11

RUFUS MOSELEY used to tell a story about a missionary who was captured by Chinese pirates. They held the old man for ransom, but he was not important enough to have someone come forward with the money demanded.

The time came when the pirate chief told the old missionary, "If the money doesn't come by tomorrow noon, we will cut off your head." The pirate chief meant it, and the missionary knew that he meant it. The old man began to prepare himself for death, and in the process of this preparation got into a high state of ecstasy. He would soon be with his Lord, and this was the greatest bliss he could imagine. He began singing hymns and loved everyone and was exceedingly kind to everybody. This caused consternation among the pirates. They could not believe it.

"Why do you act this way when you know you are going to die?" the missionary was asked. Then he told them about Jesus and the great happiness he would have when he saw Him face to face after he died. Shocked by such a revelation, the pirate chief blurted out, "If it's going to make you so happy, we won't cut off your head!" Thus the old man was saved from beheading because he rejoiced and was exceeding glad in his persecution.

The wording of this beatitude presents something of a problem. It might make more sense if it said that blessed are they who are persecuted "on my account," instead of persecuted "*falsely* on my account." To be persecuted for the sake of Jesus (because one is committed to His way of life and the application of it in society) means that one is in conformity and community with the dedication and attitudes of Jesus.

Mrs. Roland Brown reminded me that the punctuation in our English Bible reflects the judgment of the translator —that is, there is no punctuation in the original Greek. A slight change in the punctuation would make a lot of difference in the meaning.

Suppose we punctuated this beatitude to read like this: "Blessed are you when men revile and persecute you and utter all kinds of evil against you falsely. On my account, rejoice and be glad, for your reward is great in heaven, for so men persecuted the prophets who were before you." In my opinion, this makes the meaning and the intent of the beatitude more clear and justifiable. However, even as it is now written in our Bible, it can be interpreted in a manner that makes sense, and relates rightly to the personality of Jesus. If he is in community with the nature and personality of Jesus, one may well be persecuted "falsely" by the social and cultural systems of his time. Those who persecute him will feel that they are judging justly; however, their standards of justice will be false. Their standards are not the same as the standards of God. Hence, the one being judged will be judged *falsely*, according to the standards of God. His false persecution will be because of (on account of) his commitment to Jesus and His way.

Mrs. Brown's insight is in agreement with this interpretation. Her suggestion simply clarifies its meaning. One is persecuted falsely if the standards by which he is being judged are false. He will be blessed because he is a channel for the true standards of God in human affairs. But for the sake of (on account of the nature of) Jesus and all the prophets, such a man will rejoice and find gladness in the knowledge that he is in good company. At the same time, he is fulfilling the deepest desires and needs of his own godly nature, and of the image in which he is created.

The ultimate yearning of everyone is that his life will amount to something, count for something in the final analysis, and that the drained efforts and spent energies will not have been in vain. How awful to have drifted through life, compromising with the expediencies of the moment, only to find out in the end that one had missed the purpose of it all! There is an instinctive hope and belief in everyone that life does have a purpose, and that that purpose has meaning and plan and pattern—that we came from somewhere and are going somewhere, and that, over all, God is in charge of our lives.

Surely the Psalmist had something of this awareness when he wrote: "For thou didst form my inward parts, thou didst knit me together in my mother's womb. I praise thee, for thou art fearful and wonderful. Wonderful are thy works! Thou knowest me right well; my frame was not hidden from thee, when I was being made in secret, intricately wrought in the depths of the earth. Thy eyes beheld my unformed substance; in thy book were written, every one of them, the days that were formed for me, when as yet there was none of them" (PSALM 139:13-16).

One of the greatest friends I have had on this earth told me that, at a period when he was in the depths of depression, where he came from became very important to him. Somehow life after death has to be considered in connection with this other very basic question of human existence. In ways that we do not know, God had charge of the reins of our lives even before we appeared on this earth. Theologians have wrestled with the problem as to when a man becomes a soul. The human body is the vehicle for this soul, but it is not the soul. Wherever we came from, *we who are spirit*, we have an instinctive knowledge that God had a hand in it, and was in charge of it.

In Genesis 28 there is the story of Jacob running for his life. One night he lies down to sleep and has a dream. A ladder reaches from heaven to earth, and from earth to heaven, and angels are ascending and descending. Jacob looks to the top and there he sees God standing over all.

There are times in life when it is necessary for us all to have the dream of Jacob's ladder. There are times when life becomes drab and ceases to have meaning. There are times when we have lost the vision. Day after day we go through the motions of being alive while feeling as if we were dead on the inside. We demand that life should have meaning. We demand that life should be under the direction of God. We demand that God should stand on top of everything, and look down and direct things according to His own intention.

Once, at a conference, I talked about the vision of Jacob's

ladder. I emphasized the point that God was over all, and said that there comes a time in everyone's life when one is weary of living by his wits, and striving to force every circumstance into his own little orbit of self-interest. One becomes tired; one becomes bored; one becomes weary. Then comes the demand and the yearning and the cry that surely life is more than this! When one reaches the end of himself and enters into the stillness of his own soul, always there is the vision of Jacob's ladder, and always God is standing over all.

One of my very good friends came to me afterwards and said that he needed this message. Even though he was engaged in very holy and very godly work, the months and the years had drained him. He needed to be reminded of the vision, the vision for which he had entered the ministry in the beginning. Such a time comes in everybody's life. We demand to know, we yearn to know, we want to be confirmed in our belief that God is over all.

Jesus believed so, and he evidently believed that like spirits attracted like spirits. He said that those from the East and from the West would come and sit at table with Abraham in the Kingdom of God. In this way, Jesus was a Universalist. He did not say that only the Jews from the East and the West would come, or even that only the Christians from the East and the West would come and sit at table with Abraham. He said, in very plain language, that those of faith, those of similar spirit, would come from the East and the West. Regardless of their religion, or the color of their skin, or their nationality, they would sit at table with Abraham. *Spirit would recognize spirit!*

With the same viewpoint, Jesus told the people in the synagogue of His hometown that the prophet Elijah had been sent to the widow of Zarephath because he could find no spiritual response among the Israelites. *Deep would respond to deep;* and spirits on the same wave length would respond to each other, regardless of nationality and traditions.

Therefore, the ultimate joy of life is to find association in the Kingdom of God with the prophets—those who raised human aspirations by offering a clearly delineated set of standards closer to God's intention for human living. Yes, they were ridiculed, reviled, imprisoned, and sawn asunder, but the ultimate goal and worth of their lives was confirmed. To be in league with them, and therefore to *know* them, and to be known as one of them in the society of God, is success! This is the only real cause for being glad. The arrow of life has found its mark! In the words of Robert Louis Stevenson, the sailor is "home from the sea!"

A little unwanted orphan boy from Japan illustrates the pith of this beatitude. Toyohiko Kagawa was the illegitimate offspring of a well-to-do father and a dancing girl. Reared in the home of his father, he was not wanted, maybe because he was a constant reminder of the unfaithfulness of the father. The time came when the only real companionship this little boy had was out in the fields, where he found the Otherness in the form of Jesus Christ to whom he dedicated his life. Then came years of schooling, seminary at Princeton, and the return to Japan. Kagawa wrote many novels which sold in the millions of copies. He could have become independently wealthy, but he did not choose to do so.

Toyohiko Kagawa spent his money on the destitute and on the poor. He nearly lost his eyesight from a disease he contracted by living with slum dwellers. He worked and fought for the social elevation of those who had no champion. He instituted cooperatives for slum dwellers. He was beaten many times, but always he worked on, holding to the vision he had received concerning God in Jesus Christ. During the Second World War he was hunted by his own government, and had to hide out in the forests. Still, this man continued to work for his Lord. Finally he died, and today he is considered one of the saints of this age.

Toyohiko Kagawa is also to be counted with the great prophets of faith of ancient time. He is to be numbered amongst the great examples of faith which are recorded in the eleventh chapter of Hebrews: "These all died in faith, not having received what was promised, but having seen it and greeted it from afar, and having acknowledged that they were strangers and exiles on the earth. For people who speak thus make it clear that they are seeking a homeland. If they had been thinking of that land from which they had gone out, they would have had opportunity to return. But as it is, they desire a better country, that is, a heavenly one. Therefore God is not ashamed to be called their God, for he has prepared for them a city" (HEBREWS 11:13-16).

According to ordinary standards of reward and punishment, it is difficult to understand how one could be happy about being persecuted for the vision, life, and standards of Jesus of Nazareth—or, for that matter, be happy about being persecuted at all. Happiness and joy, under ordinary circumstances, are the result of being liked, loved, accepted, and praised by others, according to the normal standards of behavior and achievement in our society. One who is persecuted certainly does not meet such standards. This is the very reason for his persecution.

Therefore, for one to rejoice in persecution must mean that he is living by some other commitment and set of standards. In the context of this beatitude, he most certainly is doing so. The one who is living "on my account," for the sake of Jesus, has accepted another standard of morality and finds a joy in being true to the values to which he has committed his life. He would persecute himself if he were untrue to himself. He would feel guilty and ashamed if he were praised by others for being untrue to himself. Thus we have the Apostle Paul writing, ". . . woe is unto me, if I preach not the gospel!" (I CORINTHIANS 9:16, KJV).

Man has a need to be true to himself, regardless of the standards he has embraced. It is not unusual for a man to give himself up for perpetrating some crime to which the police have found no solution. His reason often is that life has become unbearable to him, and he feels the need of making restitution. Every so often we read in the newspapers that someone has returned stolen money anonymously, money which he had stolen many years ago. Again there is a burden of guilt which must be expiated.

True rejoicing comes about through being true to one's basic nature, through achieving according to the standards of that purpose. This results in what is known as the "integration of the human personality." William Shakespeare had an insight into the very core of human nature when he wrote, ". . . to thine own self be true . . ." (*Hamlet*). To the one who has given his life to the Person and standards of Jesus Christ, the only rejoicing possible is in being true to that Person, and to those standards.

A moving story is told about Sundar Singh, the Christian saint of India. In a village he was beaten and thrown into prison for his activities. His jailors were incensed at him for preaching when he had been commanded not to preach. They put him in a pit with stinging scorpions, and as the scorpions crawled over his body, Singh prayed and prayed to God, and entered into a state of ecstasy. He began to sing, and blessed not only the scorpions, but also his jailors. They had never seen such a man—one who would bless them when they were reviling him. They became so conscience-stricken that they released him.

Something of the same thing must have happened at the stoning of Stephen, the first Christian martyr. According to the story in the Book of Acts, he was so filled with the joy of God and the goodness of God, with the life and nature of Jesus Christ, that he prayed God to forgive those who were stoning him to death. Evidently this had a tremendous effect upon a young man who was holding the cloaks of those who were doing the stoning, for this young man later became known as the Apostle Paul.

Yes, it is possible to rejoice in persecution, but only when one is true to himself and to his Lord.

It is said that when General Booth, the founder of the Salvation Army, was an old man he had to have one of his eyes removed by surgery. His reply was typical of a completely dedicated life and an indomitable spirit. "I have served Christ for fifty years with two eyes; now I shall serve him with one eye." The circumstances of life did not determine General Booth's joy nor his loyalties. He envisioned a Kingdom and a society that *involved* this world, but which was not *of* this world.

The Apostle Paul rejoiced in his trials—being lashed forty times less one, being shipwrecked—and all of the other harshnesses and brutalities which were showered on him. Yet he was able to say, "I have learned, in whatever state I am, to be content. . . . I can do all things in him who strengthens me" (PHILIPPIANS 4:11-13).

If society as a whole, and each individual life within that society, is to be changed in order to result in an earth which is in community with God—so much in community with God that earth becomes heaven and heaven becomes earth—then it is going to take those who are willing to be judged *falsely on God's account*, in order to change mankind into a greater and lovelier image.

"Blessed are you when men revile you and persecute you and utter all kinds of evil against you falsely on My account. Rejoice and be glad . . ."—for you are the expression of the eternal and universal Heavenly Father here on earth!

Epilogue

HERE we have the rules and guidelines of great living. Perhaps they sound so simple that one is apt to believe he can appropriate them and practice them by himself. Nothing could be further from the truth.

We need more than ourselves if we are to meet the conditions of the beatitudes. We need God, and the only way we can have God is by bowing our knees in humble submission and in thankful adoration.

It is a matter of dying to self, and that can only come about in the act of reaching out and inviting Christ to reign on the throne of our hearts, and finding a new Spirit entering us. In our very weakness we find strength, in our poverty we find abundance, in our sorrow we find joy, and in our loneliness we find the Comforter.

God is the answer! Yet that answer takes search, and the search comes only through living and plumbing the depths of life. The answer is here within us, and yet beyond us. But it is here, nevertheless—closer than hands and feet.

I am alone; thou only art in Me.
I am the stream of Life that flows through thee.
I comprehend all substance, fill all space.
I am pure Being, by whom all things be.

I, God, enfold thee like an atmosphere.
Thou to thyself wert never yet more near.
Think not to shun Me: whither would'st thou fly?
Nor go not hence to seek Me: I am here.

James Rhoades

God is here. It is in the giving up of oneself and in the commitment of oneself that one finds Him. The search through the experiences of life is necessary. In the words of Sir Galahad:

So pass I hostel, hall, and grange;
By bridge and ford, by park and pale,
All-arm'd I ride, whate'er betide,
Until I find the holy Grail.

Alfred, Lord Tennyson

The answer to our search is contained in the beatitudes of Jesus. Knowing that answer is important, but it is not enough. We need the help of the Master who was the incarnation of these beatitudes, and who is willing to help us. In prayer, desire, and commitment to Him, we can have it.

When it happens, when we take His yoke upon us and learn of Him, we shall find rest unto our very souls. We will be new creatures in Christ Jesus; old things will have passed away and all things will have become new.

A native health and innocence
Within my bones did grow,
And while my God did all his Glories show,
I felt a vigour in my sense

That all was Spirit. I within did flow
    With seas of life, like wine;
I nothing in the world did know
    But 'twas divine.

                    Thomas Traherne